IMMIGRATION IN THE 21
POLITICAL, SOCIAL AND E(

REFUGEES AROUND THE WORLD

REGIONAL ASSESSMENTS, U.S. ADMISSIONS PROGRAMS AND POLICY

IMMIGRATION IN THE 21ST CENTURY: POLITICAL, SOCIAL AND ECONOMIC ISSUES

Additional books in this series can be found on Nova's website under the Series tab.

Additional e-books in this series can be found on Nova's website under the e-book tab.

IMMIGRATION IN THE 21ST CENTURY:
POLITICAL,SOCIAL AND ECONOMIC ISSUES

REFUGEES AROUND THE WORLD

REGIONAL ASSESSMENTS, U.S. ADMISSIONS PROGRAMS AND POLICY

JAROD HUMPHREY
EDITOR

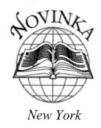

New York

Library of Congress Cataloging-in-Publication Data

ISBN: 978-1-63117-896-2

Published by Nova Science Publishers, Inc. † New York

CONTENTS

PREFACE

A refugee is a person fleeing his or her country because of persecution or a well-founded fear of persecution on account of race, religion, nationality, membership in a particular social group, or political opinion. According to the United Nations High Commissioner for Refugees (UNHCR) there are approximately 15.4 million refugees in the world. The vast majority of these refugees will receive support in the country to which they fled until they can voluntarily and safely return to their home country. A small number of refugees will be allowed to become citizens in the country to which they fled, and an even smaller number — primarily those who are at the highest risk — will be resettled in a third country. While UNHCR reports that less than 1 percent of all refugees are eventually resettled in third countries, the United States welcomes over half of these refugees, more than all other resettlement countries combined. This book provides regional overviews of the refugee situation around the globe, country conditions, data on refugees worldwide and programs for refugee admittance to the United States.

Chapter 1 – According to the United Nations High Commissioner for Refugees (UNHCR) there are approximately 15.4 million refugees in the world. The vast majority of these refugees will receive support in the country to which they fled until they can voluntarily and safely return to their home country. A small number of refugees will be allowed to become citizens in the country to which they fled, and an even smaller number — primarily those who are at the highest risk — will be resettled in a third country. While UNHCR reports that less than 1 percent of all refugees are eventually resettled in third countries, the United States welcomes over half of these refugees, more than all other resettlement countries combined.

This report provides regional overviews of the refugee situation around the globe, country conditions, data on refugees worldwide and programs for refugee admittance to the United States.

Chapter 2 – A refugee is a person fleeing his or her country because of persecution or a well-founded fear of persecution on account of race, religion, nationality, membership in a particular social group, or political opinion. Typically, the annual number of refugees that can be admitted into the United States, known as the refugee ceiling, and the allocation of these numbers by region are set by the President after consultation with Congress at the start of each fiscal year. For FY2013, the worldwide refugee ceiling is 70,000, with 67,000 admissions numbers allocated among the regions of the world and 3,000 numbers comprising an unallocated reserve. An unallocated reserve is to be used if, and where, a need develops for refugee slots in excess of the allocated numbers. The FY2013 regional allocations are, as follows: Africa (12,000), East Asia (17,000), Europe and Central Asia (2,000), Latin America/Caribbean (5,000), and Near East/South Asia (31,000).

Overseas processing of refugees is conducted through a system of three priorities for admission. Priority 1 comprises cases involving persons facing compelling security concerns. Priority 2 comprises cases involving persons from specific groups of special humanitarian concern to the United States (e.g., Iranian religious minorities). Priority 3 comprises family reunification cases involving close relatives of persons admitted as refugees or granted asylum.

Chapter 3 – Every year, the United States provides resettlement opportunities to thousands of the world's most vulnerable refugees, in a program endorsed by the President (and every President since 1980) through an annual determination. The U.S. Refugee Admissions Program (USRAP), which resettled over 58,000 refugees in the United States in 2012, reflects our own tradition as a nation of immigrants and refugees. It is an important, enduring and ongoing expression of our commitment to international humanitarian principles. The United States remains the largest resettlement country in the world, receiving more than half of all refugees resettled worldwide each year through the United Nations High Commissioner for Refugees (UNHCR).

The Bureau of Population, Refugees, and Migration (PRM) is committed to improving the effectiveness of the U.S. Refugee Admissions Program, and regularly assesses refugee populations worldwide to ensure that the program is responsive to the resettlement needs of the most vulnerable among them that require this solution.

In: Refugees Around the World
Editor: Jarod Humphrey

ISBN: 978-1-63117-896-2
© 2014 Nova Science Publishers, Inc.

Chapter 1

PROPOSED REFUGEE ADMISSIONS FOR FISCAL YEAR 2014[*]

U.S. Departments of State, Homeland Security, and Health and Human Services

PREFACE

According to the United Nations High Commissioner for Refugees (UNHCR) there are approximately 15.4 million refugees in the world. The vast majority of these refugees will receive support in the country to which they fled until they can voluntarily and safely return to their home country. A small number of refugees will be allowed to become citizens in the country to which they fled, and an even smaller number — primarily those who are at the highest risk — will be resettled in a third country. While UNHCR reports that less than 1 percent of all refugees are eventually resettled in third countries, the United States welcomes over half of these refugees, more than all other resettlement countries combined.

This report provides regional overviews of the refugee situation around the globe, country conditions, data on refugees worldwide and programs for refugee admittance to the United States.

---

[*] This is an edited, reformatted and augmented version of a report to Congress, released by the U.S. Department of State, December 19, 2013.

Report to the Congress
Submitted on Behalf of the President of the United States
To the Committees on the Judiciary United States Senate and United
States House of Representatives
In Fulfillment of the Requirements of Sections 207(D)(1) and (E) of the
Immigration and Nationality Act

INTRODUCTION

This *Proposed Refugee Admissions for Fiscal Year 2014: Report to the Congress* is submitted in compliance with Sections 207(d)(1) and (e) of the Immigration and Nationality Act (INA). The Act requires that before the start of the fiscal year and, to the extent possible, at least two weeks prior to consultations on refugee admissions, members of the Committees on the Judiciary of the Senate and the House of Representatives be provided with the following information:

1) A description of the nature of the refugee situation;
2) A description of the number and allocation of the refugees to be admitted and an analysis of conditions within the countries from which they came;
3) A description of the plans for their movement and resettlement and the estimated cost of their movement and resettlement;
4) An analysis of the anticipated social, economic, and demographic impact of their admission to the United States;[1]
5) A description of the extent to which other countries will admit and assist in the resettlement of such refugees;
6) An analysis of the impact of the participation of the United States in the resettlement of such refugees on the foreign policy interests of the United States; and
7) Such additional information as may be appropriate or requested by such members.

In addition, this report contains information as required by Section 602(d) of the International Religious Freedom Act of 1998 (Public Law 105-292, October 27, 1998, 112 Stat. 2787) (IRFA) about religious persecution of refugee populations eligible for consideration for admission to the United States. This report meets the reporting requirements of Section 305(b) of the

North Korean Human Rights Act of 2004 (Public Law 108-333, October 18, 2004, 118 Stat. 1287) by providing information about specific measures taken to facilitate access to the United States refugee program for individuals who have fled "countries of particular concern" for violations of religious freedoms, identified pursuant to Section 402(b) of the IRFA.

FOREWORD

The U.S. Refugee Admissions Program (USRAP) is a critical component of the United States' overall protection efforts around the globe. On the occasion of World Refugee Day on June 20, both President Obama and Secretary Kerry re-affirmed the U.S. commitment to helping refugees and the importance of providing safe haven in America. While starting life anew in the United States presents considerable challenges, it also creates unparalleled hope and provides opportunity for a new beginning for tens of thousands of persons each year. The support and assistance that average Americans provide to these newcomers greatly helps them integrate into our country. Refugees add to America's vitality and diversity by making substantial contributions to our economic and cultural life.

Resettlement in a third country is a durable solution for refugees who are among the most vulnerable in the world and for whom the other two durable solutions -- repatriation or local integration in the country of refuge -- are not viable options. Traditionally, the U.S. Refugee Admissions Program (USRAP) offers resettlement to refugees regardless of their location, national origin, health status, occupational skills, or level of educational attainment.

Maximizing U.S. Arrivals

Refugee arrivals in FY 2013 are up sharply from the previous two years thanks to the concerted efforts of the many partners involved in U.S. resettlement. Arrivals are on-pace to exceed FY 2012 arrivals by more than 10,000 individuals, and will come very near to reaching the President's authorized ceiling of 70,000. This success was made possible in part by better synchronization of security and medical checks for refugee families as well as investments in UNHCR's ability to refer refugees from the Middle East and Africa. The United States will welcome a record number of Iraqi refugees in 2013, thanks to staffing increases for Iraq operations and efficiencies in security checks. As of August 2013 the United States has resettled more than 88,000 Iraqis since 2007, even despite a difficult operating environment in some host countries.

Arrivals from Africa are also strong and are on-pace to exceed our regional projection of 12,000 refugees. Processing improvements in Havana have led to strong Cuban refugee arrivals, with more than 4,000 expected by the end of FY 2013.

Helping the Hard-to-Reach and the Especially Vulnerable

The Administration has worked closely with Congress to invest the resources necessary to reach the most desperate groups of refugees. These individuals may be small in number, yet they are hard to resettle because they are located in less accessible places. In FY 2013 the program will admit refugees of some 65 nationalities from sites around the world. We have interviewed and processed the cases of refugees from the Libyan-Egyptian border, the Dadaab camp in Kenya, transit centers in Europe, urban areas in Latin America, and remote camps along the Thai-Burma border, among other locations.

Through resettlement efforts targeting the most vulnerable refugees – even in hard to reach places – the United States ensures that the USRAP is consistent with humanitarian principles.

During the past year, the USRAP continued to help many of the world's most vulnerable refugees, who have lived in protracted situations for years, uncertain about their fate and unable to develop their potential. These include survivors of torture or gender-based violence, and lesbian, gay, bisexual, or transgender (LGBT) individuals.

"On World Refugee Day, the United States stands with the more than 45 million people around the world who have been forced to flee their homes due to conflict and political violence.

This year, I want especially to thank countries and communities working to meet the needs of those who have fled the ongoing violence in Syria. In word and deed, countries like Lebanon, Jordan, Turkey, Iraq, and Egypt have taken on extraordinary burdens as they host people displaced by horrific violence. We are grateful for their generosity, and pleased to support their efforts in addressing this humanitarian crisis.

Today, we reaffirm our commitment to working with the Office of the UN High Commissioner for Refugees and our partners and Allies to protect and assist all those displaced as they work to rebuild their lives in peace and dignity."

President Barack Obama
June 20, 2013
World Refugee Day

Reuniting Families

Early this past year the United States reinstated the Priority Three (P-3) family reunification program following a four-year suspension due to high levels of fraud uncovered via DNA testing. The revised program includes new anti-fraud measures, including the requirement of DNA evidence to verify certain biological relationships. These measures will mitigate attempted fraud and enable bona fide refugees to join existing family members in the United States.

Improvements to Global Resettlement

Efforts to expand the number of nations involved in the resettlement of refugees continue to pay dividends. In recent years, countries without a history of resettling refugees have stepped forward and established programs. Recent additions include France, Germany, Belgium, Portugal, Spain, the Czech Republic, and Romania. In 2012, 27 countries resettled refugees identified and referred by UNHCR.

For several years the U.S. Government has provided financial support to countries in Latin America to enhance their efforts to initiate and build resettlement programs. These efforts focus largely on the resettlement of Colombian refugees in countries that have not traditionally resettled refugees. The Department of State has also mentored the governments of Uruguay and Bulgaria in order to improve or launch their own resettlement efforts.

"Today is just the 12th official World Refugee Day, but I'm proud to say that in United States of America, our country has had a tradition of welcoming the "huddled masses yearning to breathe free," and it runs deep in our roots. I think it's safe to say it's part of our DNA as Americans, and we're proud of that.

Roughly 150 years before the American Revolution took place and 400 years before the Statue of Liberty first stood up in New York Harbor to welcome people, a fellow by the name of John Winthrop came to this land as a Puritan refugee from England with a group of refugees on a sail vessel, the Arbella.

And he crossed the Atlantic. Before he arrived in Boston Harbor, he delivered a very well-known sermon, envisioning the colony they were going to create there as this "City Upon a Hill," words that have been well quoted now by President Kennedy initially and President Reagan subsequently. He challenged the congregation that came over with him to serve as a model of justice and tolerance because, as he said, "the eyes of all people are upon us."

Well, I would say to you today that they still are. The eyes of all people are upon us. And opening our docks and our doors to refugees has been part of the great tradition of our country. It defines us. It really is who we are. Most people came to this country at one point or another from another place."

Secretary John Kerry
June 20, 2013
World Refugee Day

Enhancing America's Security While Welcoming Bona Fide Refugees

In the last several years, the USRAP incorporated additional security enhancements to safeguard the resettlement program from fraud and national security risks. The Administration also continued to work over the past year to address the effects of the broad definitions of "terrorist activity" and "terrorist organization" under U.S. immigration law on refugees and other immigrants whose admission to or presence in the United States does not compromise our national security and is consistent with U.S. foreign policy interests.

Over the course of the past year, US Citizenship and Immigration Services (USCIS) has continued to implement several group-based and situational exemptions authorized by Department of Homeland Security Secretary Napolitano. As of July 2013, USCIS has granted more than 400 exemptions from terrorism-related inadmissibility grounds for refugee applicants in FY 2013, after examining each on a case-by-case basis to determine that their admission would not compromise our national security.

Ensuring a Suitable Welcome

In FY 2010 the Department of State increased the per capita Reception and Placement grant from $900 to $1,800. This grant helps cover initial services after a refugee's arrival in the United States. This step recognized that the grant amount was insufficient and had not kept pace with inflation, the cost of living and the rising costs of resettlement. The doubling of this grant was undertaken with the approval of and support from Congress. In FY 2013 the per capita grant increased again to $1,875 in line with realistic estimates of needs.

In FY 2013, the Department of State maintained a policy that provides resettlement agencies a guaranteed minimum amount of funding so that they can provide quality reception and placement services to arriving refugees even if a lower than expected number of refugees are admitted or if there are unavoidable delays in arrivals. The Department expects to continue this funding mechanism in FY 2014.

In addition to the Reception and Placement grant provided by the State Department, the Office of Refugee Resettlement at the Department of Health and Human Services (HHS/ORR) funds time-limited assistance programs (up to eight months from arrival) and social service programs (up to five years) that provide benefits and services to refugees. These programs assist refugees in finding employment in order to become economically self-sufficient and with social integration. Recently, HHS/ORR has worked to support intensive case management to ensure that refugees have the best opportunities for success by ensuring supportive longer-term relationships and developing self-sufficiency plans based on refugees' individual strengths.

The State Department and HHS/ORR continue to work closely with receiving communities to ensure stakeholders have the tools and information to ensure the best possible welcome and support for newly arrived refugees. Over the past year consultations took place in Arizona, California, Colorado,

Connecticut, Florida, Georgia, Indiana, Maine, Michigan, Minnesota, Nevada, Ohio, Pennsylvania, Tennessee, and Washington, D.C. Moreover, ORR has recently announced the establishment of regional offices in order to increase engagement and consultation with resettlement stakeholders. The Administration will continue to explore ways of sustaining a strong federal-state-community partnership and ensuring that refugees are able to integrate successfully in the United States.

Resettlement As a Key Part of an Overall Approach

Overseas, the U.S. Government continues to use resettlement as one part of an overall approach that aims to demonstrate U.S. commitment and leadership and promote more generous policies among (a) countries of origin, (b) refugee hosting countries and (c) other resettlement countries.

UNHCR has identified seven priority situations where it believes third-country resettlement to be the key to unlocking other measures to help refugees stuck in protracted situations. The USRAP has resettled considerable numbers of these refugees, particularly Iraqis living in Syria, Jordan and Lebanon; Iraqis and Iranians in Turkey; Afghans in Iran; Somalis in Kenya; and Colombians in Ecuador. The United States is now chairing a group of countries that will participate in UNHCR's latest priority situation, the resettlement of 50,000 Congolese from Uganda, Rwanda, Burundi, and Tanzania. In addition, the U.S. continues to build the capacity of new resettlement countries, thereby creating more resettlement slots for vulnerable refugees.

Planning for the Future

Large-scale processing of Congolese refugees by the United States will ensue in FY 2014, as UNHCR and the international resettlement community gear up to resettle 50,000 Congolese in coming years. Small-scale resettlement of Darfuri refugees in Chad, another group in a protracted situation, should re-commence in FY 2014. UNHCR has begun a discussion with the United States and other governments on resettling particularly vulnerable Syrian refugees, such as victims of gender-based violence and/or torture and some medical cases, likely to begin in FY 2014. Programs for Burmese refugees in Thailand and Bhutanese refugees in Nepal will begin to wind down in the next few years, as the groups eligible for these programs have largely availed themselves of resettlement opportunities to the United States or another country. Refugee resettlement will continue to be an essential component of the U.S. Government's response to refugee protection needs for years to come and will continue to adapt to meet changing refugee needs.

I. OVERVIEW OF U.S. REFUGEE POLICY

At the end of 2012, the estimated refugee population worldwide stood at 15.4 million, with 10.5 million receiving protection or assistance from the United Nations High Commissioner for Refugees (UNHCR). The United States actively supports efforts to provide protection, assistance, and durable solutions to these refugees, as these measures fulfill our humanitarian interests and further our foreign policy and national security interests. Under the authority of the Migration and Refugee Assistance Act of 1962, as amended, the United States contributes to the programs of UNHCR, the International Committee of the Red Cross (ICRC), the International Organization for Migration (IOM), the United Nations Relief and Works Agency for Palestine Refugees in the Near East (UNRWA), and other international and non-governmental organizations that provide protection and assistance to refugees, internally displaced persons (IDPs), victims of conflict, stateless persons, and other vulnerable migrants. These contributions are used to address the legal and physical protection needs of refugees and to furnish basic assistance such as water, sanitation, food, health care, shelter, education, and other services. The United States monitors these programs to ensure the most effective use of resources, maximizing humanitarian impact for the beneficiaries.

The United States and UNHCR recognize that most refugees desire safe, voluntary return to their homeland as their preferred solution. During FY 2013, the United States continued to support voluntary repatriation programs around the world. Refugee repatriation operations brought refugees home to Afghanistan, Burundi, Cote d'Ivoire, the Democratic Republic of Congo (DRC), and Sri Lanka. These operations were carried out to protect returning refugees as well as to help them contribute to the stabilization, reconstruction, and development of their home countries.

Where opportunities for return remain elusive, the United States and partners pursue self-sufficiency and temporary, indefinite, or permanent local integration in countries of asylum. The Department of State encourages host governments to protect refugees and allow them to integrate into local communities. The State Department further promotes local integration by funding programs to enhance refugee self-sufficiency and support community-based social services. Groups that may avail themselves of opportunities for local integration include Afghans in India, Angolans in Zambia, Burundians in Tanzania, Eritreans in Sudan, Liberians and Sierra Leoneans in seven countries across West Africa, and Colombians in Ecuador, Costa Rica, Panama and Venezuela.

UNHCR estimates that there are 12 million people worldwide who are not recognized nationals of any state and are, therefore, legally or de facto stateless. Without recognized citizenship in any country, many stateless persons exist in refugee-like situations, unable to claim rights and denied even the most basic protections of law. The United States has supported UNHCR's efforts to prevent and reduce statelessness, including addressing gaps in citizenship laws, eliminating provisions that discriminate against women, and promoting fair application of those laws. U.S. contributions to UNHCR's core budget support efforts to prevent and address statelessness in Burma, the Dominican Republic, Kuwait, Nepal, Sudan, Turkmenistan, and elsewhere.

In addition, the Department of State seeks to use the U.S. Refugee Admissions Program (USRAP) to demonstrate U.S. leadership while encouraging other countries to do more to help stateless people and refugees stuck in protracted situations. This approach is reflected in the current resettlement of Rohingya refugees, as well as in past resettlement of Meskhetian Turks. The Bureau of Population, Refugees, and Migration (PRM) also uses diplomacy to mobilize other governments to prevent and resolve situations of statelessness. For example, over the past year PRM has conducted field missions and monitored the situations confronting stateless people in Burma, Kuwait, and Nepal. Diplomatic efforts include U.S. sponsorship of the July 2012 UN Human Rights Council resolution on the rights to a nationality for women and children, as part of the Department's efforts to combat discrimination against women in nationality laws.

The United States and UNHCR recognize that resettlement in third countries is a vital tool for providing refugees protection and/or durable solutions in some particularly difficult cases. For some refugees, resettlement is the best, and perhaps the only, alternative. Stateless refugees who arrive in the United States for resettlement not only find a durable solution to their displacement, but are also placed on a path that will afford the opportunity to naturalize and resolve their stateless status.

For more than a decade, the U.S. Government has provided financial support to expand and improve UNHCR's resettlement capacity, principally through staffing complements and facility construction. As a result, UNHCR has substantially increased referrals to the United States and other resettlement countries. We plan to continue to work with UNHCR and consult with host governments on group referrals. We will continue to assess resettlement needs and allow qualified NGOs to refer refugee applicants to the program.

The United States has also supported UNHCR's efforts to expand the number of countries active in resettlement. In 2012, UNHCR referred refugees to 27 countries for resettlement consideration. Over 90 percent were referred to the United States, Australia, and Canada. Smaller numbers of referrals were made to Argentina, Brazil, Chile, Czech Republic, Denmark, Estonia, Finland, France, Germany, Hungary, Iceland, Ireland, Italy, Netherlands, New Zealand, Norway, Portugal, Republic of Korea, Slovakia, Spain, Sweden, Switzerland, Uruguay, and the United Kingdom.

While the overall number of refugees referred by UNHCR and the percentage resettled by various countries fluctuate from year to year, the United States aims to ensure at least 50 percent of all refugees referred by UNHCR worldwide are considered for resettlement in the United States, depending on the availability of funds. Some 76 percent of UNHCR-referred refugees who were resettled in 2012, were resettled in the United States (see Table 8).

The foreign policy and humanitarian interests of the United States are often advanced by addressing refugee issues in first asylum and resettlement countries. In some cases, the United States has been able to use its leadership position in resettlement to promote and secure other durable solutions for refugees, or advance other human rights or foreign policy objectives. The United States is by far the largest single donor to UNHCR, providing over $775 million in FY 2012. During the past few years, U.S. resettlement efforts in Africa, the Middle East, and East Asia have helped energize efforts by UNHCR and other countries to ensure that first asylum is maintained for larger refugee populations or that local integration or third country resettlement are options offered to those in need. In certain locations, the prompt resettlement of politically sensitive cases has helped defuse regional tensions. In the case of refugees fleeing fighting in Libya, the U.S. was willing to resettle third-country national refugees who had fled to Tunisia and Egypt. The U.S. decision to assist ensured that the process proceeded apace and did not negatively affect the receiving countries' abilities to manage their own democratic transitions.

During its history, the USRAP has responded to changing circumstances. Even before the events of September 11, 2001, the end of the Cold War dramatically altered the context in which the USRAP operated. The program shifted its focus away from large groups concentrated in a few locations (primarily refugees from Vietnam, the former Soviet Union, and the former Yugoslavia) and began to admit refugees representing over 50 nationalities per year. Interviews of refugees by American officials from the Department of Homeland Security's U.S. Citizenship and Immigration Services (USCIS) are often conducted in remote locations and are geared toward populations in greatest need of third country resettlement opportunities.

While maintaining the United States' leadership role in humanitarian protection, an integral part of this mission is to ensure that refugee resettlement opportunities go to those who are eligible for such protection and do not present a risk to the safety and security of our country. Accordingly, the USRAP is committed to deterring and detecting fraud among those seeking to resettle in the United States and continues to employ the most rigorous security measures possible to protect against risks to our national security.

Refugees resettled in the United States enrich our nation. The USRAP is premised on the idea that refugees should become economically self-sufficient as quickly as possible. The Department of State works domestically with agencies participating in the Reception and Placement (R&P) program to ensure that refugees receive services in the first thirty to ninety days after arrival in accordance with established standards. During and after the initial resettlement period, the Office of Refugee Resettlement at the Department of Health and Human Services (HHS/ORR) provides leadership, technical assistance, and funding to states, the District of Columbia, and nonprofit organizations to help refugees to become self sufficient and integrated into U.S. society. ORR programs use formula and discretionary grants to provide cash and medical assistance, employment and training programs, and other services to newly arriving and recently arrived refugees. Moreover, refugees are Americans in waiting upon arrival. Refugees are eligible for lawful employment upon arrival in the United States. After one year, a refugee is required to apply for adjustment of status to lawful permanent resident. Five years after admission, a refugee who has been granted lawful permanent resident status is eligible to apply for citizenship.

A number of factors create challenges for resettlement agencies striving to meet the needs of refugees in the program. The refugee population is ever more linguistically diverse, with wide-ranging educational and employment histories. To better prepare refugees for arrival in the United States, the USRAP continues to improve overseas cultural orientation, including thorough curricula review and teacher training. In 2013, we conducted a second round of pilot English as a Second Language classes for some refugees in Kenya, Thailand, and Nepal. By introducing the study of English overseas, these classes are intended to provide basic English competency and promote continued language learning after arrival in the United States.

II. REFUGEE ADMISSIONS PROGRAM FOR FY 2014

Proposed Ceilings

Table 1. Refugee Admissions in FY 2012 and FY 2013, Proposed Refugee Admissions by Region for FY 2014[2]

REGION	FY 2012 ACTUAL ARRIVALS	FY 2013 CEILING	FY 2013 PROJECTED ARRIVALS	PROPOSED FY2014 CEILING
Africa	10,608	12,000	15,000	14,000
East Asia	14,366	17,000	17,000	14,000
Europe and Central Asia	1,129	2,000	1,000	1,000
Latin America/Caribbean	2,078	5,000	4,500	5,000
Near East/South Asia	30,057	31,000	32,000	34,000
Regional Subtotal	58,238	67,000	69,500	68,000
Unallocated Reserve		3,000		2,000
Total	58,238	70,000	69,500	70,000

Generally, to be considered a refugee, a person must be outside his or her country of nationality or, if stateless, outside his or her country of last habitual residence. Under the Immigration and Nationality Act (INA) § 101(a)(42)(B), however, the President may specify circumstances under which individuals who are within their countries of nationality or last habitual residence may be considered a refugee for purposes of admission to the United States. The FY 2014 proposal recommends continuing such in-country processing for specified groups in Iraq, Cuba, Eurasia and the Baltics. Persons for whom resettlement is requested by a U.S. ambassador in any location in the world may also be considered, with the understanding that they will only be referred to the USRAP following Department of State consultation with USCIS at the Department of Homeland Security (DHS).

Unallocated Reserve

This proposal includes 2,000 unallocated admissions numbers to be used if needed for additional refugee admissions from any region. The unallocated numbers would only be used following notification to Congress.

Admissions Procedures

Eligibility Criteria

The Department of State's Bureau of Population, Refugees, and Migration (PRM) is responsible for coordinating and managing the USRAP. A critical part of this responsibility is determining which individuals or groups from among the millions of refugees worldwide will have access to U.S. resettlement consideration. PRM coordinates within the Department of State, as well as with DHS/USCIS and other agencies, in carrying out this responsibility.

Section 207(a)(3) of the INA states that the USRAP shall allocate admissions among refugees "of special humanitarian concern to the United States in accordance with a determination made by the President after appropriate consultation." Which individuals are "of special humanitarian concern" to the United States for the purpose of refugee resettlement consideration is determined through the USRAP priority system. There are currently three priorities or categories of cases:

- Priority 1 – Individual cases referred to the program by virtue of their circumstances and apparent need for resettlement;
- Priority 2 – Groups of cases designated as having access to the program by virtue of their circumstances and apparent need for resettlement;
- Priority 3 – Individual cases from designated nationalities granted access for purposes of reunification with anchor family members already in the United States.

(Note: Refugees resettled in the United States may also seek the admission of spouses and unmarried children under 21 who are still abroad by filing a "Following to Join" petition, which obviates the need for a separate refugee claim adjudication. This option is described in more detail in the discussion of Visa 93 below.)

Access to the program under one of the above-listed processing priorities does not mean an applicant meets the statutory definition of "refugee" or is admissible to the United States under the INA. The ultimate determination as to whether an applicant can be admitted as a refugee is made by DHS/USCIS in accordance with criteria set forth in the INA and various security protocols. Applicants who are eligible for access within the established priorities are presented to DHS/USCIS officers for interview.

Although the access categories to the USRAP are referred to as "processing priorities," it is important to note that entering the program under a certain priority does not establish precedence in the order in which cases will be processed. Once cases are established as eligible for access under one of the three processing priorities, they all undergo the same processing steps.

Priority 1 – Individual Referrals

Priority 1 (P-1) allows consideration of refugee claims from persons of any nationality[3], usually with compelling protection needs, for whom resettlement appears to be the appropriate durable solution. Priority 1 cases are identified and referred to the program by UNHCR, a U.S. Embassy, or a designated NGO. UNHCR, which has the international mandate worldwide to provide protection to refugees, has historically referred the vast majority of cases under this priority. Some NGOs providing humanitarian assistance in locations where there are large concentrations of refugees have also undergone training by PRM and DHS/USCIS and have been designated eligible to provide Priority 1 referrals.

Process for Priority 1 Individual Referral Applications

Priority 1 referrals from UNHCR and NGOs are generally submitted to the appropriate Regional Refugee Coordinator, who forwards the referrals to the appropriate Resettlement Support Center (RSC[4]) for case processing and scheduling of the DHS/USCIS interview. PRM's Office of Admissions reviews embassy referrals for completeness and may consult with DHS in considering these referrals.

A U.S. ambassador may make a Priority 1 referral for persons still in their country of origin if the ambassador determines that such cases are in need of exceptional treatment and the Departments of State (PRM) and Homeland Security (USCIS) concur. In some cases, a Department of State request to DHS/USCIS for parole may be a more appropriate option.

Priority 2 – Group Referrals

Priority 2 (P-2) includes specific groups (within certain nationalities, clans or ethnic groups, sometimes in specified locations) identified by the Department of State in consultation with DHS/USCIS, NGOs, UNHCR, and other experts as being in need of resettlement. Some Priority 2 groups are processed in their country of origin. The process of identifying the group and its characteristics includes consideration of whether the group is of special humanitarian concern to the United States and whether members of the group will likely be able to qualify for admission as refugees under U.S. law. Groups may be designated as Priority 2 during the course of the year as circumstances dictate, and the need for resettlement arises. PRM plays the coordinating role for all group referrals to the USRAP.

There are two distinct models of Priority 2 access to the program: open access and predefined group access, normally upon the recommendation of UNHCR. Under both models, Priority 2 designations are made based on shared characteristics that define the group. In general, the possession of these characteristics is the reason the group has been persecuted in the past or faces persecution in the future.

The open-access model for Priority 2 group referrals allows individuals to seek access to the program on the basis of meeting designated criteria. To establish an open-access Priority 2 group, PRM, in consultation with DHS/USCIS, and (as appropriate) with UNHCR and others, defines the specific criteria for access. Once the designation is in place, applicants may approach the program at any of the processing locations specified as available for the group to begin the application process. Applicants must demonstrate that they meet specified criteria to establish eligibility for inclusion.

The open-access model has functioned well in the in-country programs, including the long-standing programs in Eurasia and the Baltics, and in Cuba. It was also used successfully for Vietnamese for nearly thirty years (1980-2009), Bosnian refugees during the 1990s, and is now in use for Iranian religious minorities and Iraqis with links to the United States.

The RSCs responsible for handling open-access Priority 2 applications, working under the direction of PRM, make a preliminary determination as to whether the applicants qualify for access and should be presented to DHS/USCIS for interview. Applicants who clearly do not meet the access requirements are "screened out" prior to DHS/USCIS interview.

In contrast to an open-access group, a predefined group designation is normally based on a UNHCR recommendation that lays out eligibility criteria that should apply to individuals in a specific location. Once PRM has established the access eligibility criteria for the group, in consultation with DHS/USCIS, the referring entity (usually UNHCR) provides the bio data of eligible refugee applicants for processing. This type of group referral is advantageous in situations in which the intensive labor required to generate individual referrals would be impracticable, potentially harmful to applicants due to delays, or counterproductive. Often, predefined groups are composed of persons with similar persecution claims. The predefined group referral process saves steps and can conserve scarce resources, particularly for UNHCR. In recent years, predefined groups have included certain Burmese in Thailand, certain Bhutanese in Nepal, and certain Eritreans in Ethiopia. Predefined group referrals with clear, well-defined eligibility criteria and several methods for cross-checking group membership can serve as a fraud deterrent as well, preventing non-group members from gaining access to the USRAP by falsely claiming group membership. It can also speed the resettlement process in cases where immediate protection concerns are present.

FY 2014 Priority 2 Designations

In-Country Processing Programs

The following ongoing programs that process individuals still in their country of origin under Priority 2 group designations will continue in FY 2013:

Eurasia and the Baltics

This Priority 2 designation applies to Jews, Evangelical Christians, and Ukrainian Catholic and Orthodox religious adherents identified in the Lautenberg Amendment, Public Law No. 101-167, § 599D, 103 Stat. 1261 (1989), as amended ("Lautenberg Amendment"), with close family in the United States. With annual renewal of the Lautenberg Amendment, these individuals are considered under a reduced evidentiary standard for establishing a well-founded fear of persecution.

Cuba

Included in this Priority 2 program are human rights activists, members of persecuted religious minorities, former political prisoners, forced-labor conscripts, persons deprived of their professional credentials or subjected to other disproportionately harsh or discriminatory treatment resulting from their perceived or actual political or religious beliefs or activities, and persons who have experienced or fear harm because of their relationship – family or social – to someone who falls under one of the preceding categories.

Iraqis Associated with the United States
Under various Priority 2 designations, including those set forth in the Refugee Crisis in Iraq Act, employees of the U.S. Government, a U.S. government-funded contractor or grantee, U.S. media or U.S. NGOs working in Iraq, and certain family members of such employees, as well as beneficiaries of approved I-130 (immigrant visa) petitions, are eligible for refugee processing in Iraq.

Groups of Humanitarian Concern outside the Country of Origin
The following Priority 2 groups are already designated and, in most cases, undergoing processing with significant arrivals anticipated during FY 2013. (Additional Priority 2 groups may be designated over the course of the year.)

Ethnic Minorities and others from Burma in camps in Thailand
Under this existing Priority 2 designation, individuals who have fled Burma and who are registered in nine refugee camps along the Thai/Burma border and who are identified by UNHCR as in need of resettlement are eligible for processing.

Ethnic Minorities from Burma in Malaysia
Under this Priority 2 designation, ethnic minorities from Burma who are recognized by UNHCR as refugees in Malaysia and identified as being in need of resettlement are eligible for processing.

Bhutanese in Nepal
Under this existing Priority 2 designation, Bhutanese refugees registered by UNHCR in camps in Nepal and identified as in need of resettlement are eligible for processing.

Iranian Religious Minorities
Under this Priority 2 designation, Iranian members of certain religious minorities are eligible for processing and are considered under a reduced evidentiary standard for establishing a well-founded fear of persecution, pursuant to annual renewal of the Lautenberg Amendment as amended in 2004

by Sec. 213, Division E, of the Consolidated Appropriations Act of 2004, P.L. 108-199 ("the Specter Amendment").

Iraqis Associated with the United States

Under various Priority 2 designations, including those set forth in the Refugee Crisis in Iraq Act, employees of the U.S. government, a U.S. government-funded contractor or grantee, U.S. media or U.S. NGOs working in Iraq, and certain family members of such employees, as well as beneficiaries of approved I-130 (immigrant visa) petitions, are eligible for refugee processing. This program is operating in Jordan and Egypt, in addition to the in-country program in Iraq.

Congolese in Rwanda

Under this new Priority 2 designation, certain Congolese refugees in Rwanda who were verifiably registered in 1997 and identified as in need of resettlement are eligible for processing.

Priority 3 – Family Reunification

The Priority 3 (P-3) category affords USRAP access to members of designated nationalities who have immediate family members in the United States who initially entered as refugees or were granted asylum. At the beginning of each fiscal year, PRM, in consultation with DHS/USCIS, establishes the list of nationalities eligible for processing under this priority. The PRM Assistant Secretary may modify the list during the year, in consultation with DHS/USCIS, but additions or deletions are generally made to coincide with the fiscal year.

Inclusion on the P-3 list represents a finding by PRM that the nationality is of special humanitarian concern to the United States for the purpose of family-reunification refugee processing. Eligible nationalities are selected following careful review of several factors. UNHCR's annual assessment of refugees in need of resettlement, provides insight into ongoing refugee situations, which could create the need for family-reunification processing. In addition, prospective or ongoing repatriation efforts and U.S. foreign policy interests must be weighed in determining which nationalities should be eligible.

The P-3 program has undergone significant changes in recent years. In order to qualify for access under P-3 procedures, an applicant must have been outside of his or her country of origin, have had an Affidavit of Relationship

(AOR) filed on his or her behalf by an eligible "anchor" relative in the United States during a period in which the nationality was included on the eligibility list, and have been cleared for onward processing by the DHS/USCIS Refugee Access Verification Unit (RAVU).

The following family members of the U.S.-based anchor are qualified for inclusion on the case: spouses, unmarried children under 21, and/or parents. Qualifying anchors are persons who were admitted to the United States as refugees or were granted asylum, including persons who are lawful permanent residents or U.S. citizens who initially were admitted to the United States as refugees or were granted asylum.

In addition to the qualifying family members of a U.S.-based anchor listed above, on a case-by-case basis, an individual may be added on to a P-3 case if that individual:

1) lived in the same household as the Qualifying Family Member in the country of nationality or, if stateless, last habitual residence; and
2) was part of the same economic unit as the Qualifying Family Member in the country of nationality or, if stateless, last habitual residence; and
3) demonstrates exceptional and compelling humanitarian circumstances that justify inclusion on the Qualifying Family Member's case.

These individuals "are not "spouses" or "children", under INA 207(c)(2)(A)" and thus cannot derive their refugee status from the Principal Applicant. They must, therefore, independently establish that they qualify as a refugee.

In March 2008, in consultation with DHS/USCIS, PRM suspended P-3 processing and issued a moratorium on P-3 arrivals from certain processing locations due to indications of extremely high rates of fraud in claimed family relationships identified through pilot DNA testing. Further, in October 2008, PRM suspended the acceptance of AORs of all nationalities while PRM and DHS/USCIS examined whether additional procedures could be incorporated into P-3 processing to detect and deter fraud in the future.

On October 15, 2012, we resumed P-3 processing with a newly approved AOR that is an official Department of State form (DS-7656); contains new language about penalties for committing fraud; and alerts filers that DNA evidence of certain claimed biological parent-child relationships will be required in order to gain access to a USCIS interview for refugee admission to the United States through the P-3 program. PRM and USCIS have worked closely with domestic resettlement agency partners to ensure they are aware of the changes to the form and the P-3 program, and have provided training so that they can educate their own affiliate staff on completion of the new AOR. Similarly, we have worked closely with our overseas Resettlement Support Centers to ensure that rigorous DNA collection and chain of custody procedures are in place. As of June 30, we have received more than 1,000 AORs that are in various stages of processing, mostly in East Africa. None of these cases are expected to arrive in the United States until 2014.

FY 2014 Priority 3 Nationalities

P-3 processing is available to individuals of the following nationalities:
Afghanistan
Bhutan
Burma
Burundi
Central African Republic
Colombia
Cuba
Democratic People's Republic of Korea (DPRK)
Democratic Republic of Congo (DRC)
Eritrea
Ethiopia
Haiti
Iran
Iraq
Mali
Republic of Congo (ROC)
Somalia
South Sudan
Sri Lanka
Sudan
Syria
Uzbekistan

Visa 93 – Family Reunification Following-to-Join Petitions

Under 8 CFR Section 207, a principal refugee admitted to the United States may request following-to-join benefits for his or her spouse and/or unmarried children under the age of 21 if the family has become separated. Once in the United States, and within two years of admission, the refugee may file a Form I730 Refugee/Asylee Relative Petition[5] with DHS/USCIS for each eligible family member. If the Form I-730 petition is approved by DHS/USCIS (signifying adequate proof of a qualifying family relationship), the National Visa Center then forwards the petition for travel document processing to the embassy or consulate nearest to the location of the beneficiary.

Cases gaining access to the USRAP through an approved I-730 petition are interviewed by DHS/USCIS or consular officers to verify the relationships claimed in the petition, as well as to examine any applicable bars to status and admissibility to the United States. The beneficiaries are not required to demonstrate persecution claims, as they derive their status from the refugee relative in the United States who filed the petition. Beneficiaries of I-730 petitions may be processed within their country of origin or in other locations. In 2011, USCIS and the Department of State launched a pilot program to test new procedures to increase the efficiency, consistency, and security of overseas processing of I-730 Refugee/Asylee Relative Petitions. The program was further expanded in 2013.

Anchor relatives in the United States may file an I-730 Refugee/Asylee Relative Petition and seek Priority 3 access (if eligible) simultaneously. In some cases, the I-730 will be the only option as the family members are still in their country of origin. It is also important to note that the I-730 or "follow-to-join" process does not allow the relative in the United States to petition for parents as the P-3 process does.

DHS/USCIS Refugee Adjudications

Section 207(c) of the INA grants the Secretary of the Department of Homeland Security authority to admit, at his/her discretion, any refugee who is not firmly resettled in a third country, who is determined to be of special humanitarian concern, and who is admissible to the United States. The authority to determine eligibility for refugee status has been delegated to USCIS. Beginning in FY 2006, DHS/USCIS restructured the Refugee Affairs Division and established the Refugee Corps, a specially trained cadre of officers dedicated to adjudicating applications for refugee status. The Refugee Corps provides DHS/USCIS with the necessary resources and flexibility to respond to an increasingly diversified refugee admissions program. DHS/USCIS has also substantially enhanced its security vetting, anti-fraud, and training capacity related to refugee processing.

The Eligibility Determination

In order to be approved as a refugee, an applicant must meet the refugee definition contained in § 101(a)(42) of the INA. That section provides that a refugee is a person who is outside his or her country of nationality or last habitual residence and is unable or unwilling to return to that country because of persecution or a well-founded fear of persecution on account of race, religion, nationality, membership in a particular social group, or political opinion. As mentioned above, the President may specify special circumstances under which a person can meet the refugee definition when he or she is still within the country of rigin. The definition excludes a person who has ordered, incited, assisted, or otherwise participated in persecution on account of race, religion, nationality, membership in a particular social group, or political opinion. Further, an applicant who has been "firmly resettled" in a third country may not be admitted as a refugee under INA Section207. Applicants are also subject to various statutory grounds of inadmissibility, including criminal, security, and public health grounds, some of which may be waived or from which applicants may be exempted.

The grounds of ineligibility that apply to refugee applicants include the broad terrorism-related inadmissibility grounds (TRIG) at Section 212(a)(3)(B) of the INA. Beginning in 2006, the Departments of Homeland Security, State, and Justice began to exercise a discretionary Secretarial authority to exempt certain categories of refugee applicants from TRIG inadmissibility based on a determination that they did not represent a threat to the United States and otherwise merited an exemption for humanitarian purposes. As of May 2013, more than 11,890 TRIG exemptions have been granted to refugee applicants.[6]

A DHS/USCIS officer conducts a non-adversarial, face-to-face interview of each refugee applicant designed to elicit information about the applicant's claim for refugee status and any grounds of ineligibility. The officer asks questions about the applicant's experiences in the country of origin, including problems and fears about returning (or remaining), as well as questions concerning the applicant's activities, background, and criminal history. The officer also considers evidence about conditions in the country of origin and assesses the applicant's credibility and claim.

Background Checks

Refugee applicants of all nationalities are required to undergo background security checks. Security checks include biographic name checks for all refugee applicants and biometric (fingerprint) checks for refugee applicants aged 14 to 79. PRM, through its overseas Resettlement Support Centers, initiates required biographic name checks, while USCIS is responsible for collecting biometric data for screening. Biographic and biometric information is vetted against a broad array of law enforcement, intelligence community, and other relevant databases to help confirm identity, to check for any criminal or other derogatory information (including watchlist information), and to identify information that could inform lines of questioning during the interview. Refugee applicants must clear all required security checks prior to final approval of their application.

In late 2010, the USRAP implemented an enhanced security check requirement for all refugee applicants. While implementing the enhanced check was critical to strengthening the integrity of the program, refugee admissions were disrupted in FY 2011 and FY 2012. Interagency coordination and processing procedures were improved, however, resulting in increased refugee admissions levels beginning in May 2012. Admissions levels continued at these higher levels in FY 2013.

Processing Activities of the Department of State

Overseas Processing Services

In most processing locations, PRM engages an NGO, an international organization (IO), or U.S. embassy contractors to manage a Resettlement Support Center (RSC) that assists in the processing of refugees for admission to the United States. RSC staff pre-screen applicants to determine preliminarily if they qualify for one of the applicable processing priorities and to prepare cases for DHS/USCIS adjudication. The RSCs assist applicants in completing documentary requirements and schedule DHS/USCIS refugee eligibility interviews. If an applicant is conditionally approved for resettlement, RSC staff guide the refugee through post-adjudication steps, including obtaining medical screening exams and attending cultural orientation programs. The RSC obtains sponsorship assurances and, once all required steps are completed, refers the case to IOM for transportation to the United States.

In FY 2013, NGOs (Church World Service, Hebrew Immigrant Aid Society, and International Rescue Committee) worked under cooperative agreements with PRM as RSCs at locations in Austria (covering Austria only), Kenya (covering sub-Saharan Africa), and Thailand (covering East Asia). International organizations and NGOs (IOM and the International Catholic

Migration Commission) support refugee processing activities based in Ecuador, Jordan, Russia, Nepal, and Turkey covering Latin America, the Middle East, South and Central Asia, and Europe. The U.S. Department of State supports refugee processing in Havana, Cuba.

Cultural Orientation

The Department of State strives to ensure that refugees who are accepted for admission to the United States are prepared for the profound life changes they will experience by providing cultural orientation programs prior to departure for the United States. It is critical that refugees arrive with a realistic idea of what their new lives will be like, what services will be available to them, and what their responsibilities will be.

Every refugee family receives *Welcome to the United States*, a resettlement guidebook developed with contributions from refugee resettlement workers, resettled refugees, and government officials. In 2013 the *Welcome* guide was completely revised to support overseas and domestic cultural orientation. The previous edition is still available in 15 languages: Albanian, Amharic, Arabic, Bosnian/Croatian/Serbian, Farsi, French, Karen, Kirundi, Nepali, Russian, Somali, Spanish, Swahili, Tigrinya, and Vietnamese while the new edition in available in English with translations in process. Through this book, refugees have access to accurate information about the initial resettlement period before they arrive. The *Welcome to the United States* refugee orientation video is available in 13 languages: Arabic, English, Farsi, Hmong, Karen, Karenni, Kirundi, Nepali, Russian, Somali, Spanish, Swahili, and Tigrinya. In addition, the Department of State funds one- to five-day pre-departure orientation classes for eligible refugees at sites throughout the world. In an effort to further bridge the information gap for certain groups, brief video presentations featuring the experience of recently resettled refugees of the same ethnic group are made available to refugee applicants overseas.

Transportation

The Department of State funds the international transportation of refugees resettled in the United States through a program administered by IOM. The cost of transportation is provided to refugees in the form of a loan. Refugees are responsible for repaying these loans over time, beginning six months after their arrival, although it is possible to request a deferral based on inability to begin paying at six months.

Reception and Placement (R&P)

In FY 2013, PRM funded cooperative agreements with nine private voluntary agencies to provide initial resettlement services to refugees arriving in the United States. The R&P agencies are responsible for providing initial reception and core services (including housing, furnishings, clothing and food, as well as assistance with access to medical, employment, educational, and social services) to arriving refugees. These services are provided according to standards of care within a framework of outcomes and indicators developed jointly by the NGO community, state refugee coordinators, and U.S. government agencies. The nine organizations maintain a nationwide network of some 350 affiliated offices to provide services. Two of the organizations also maintain a network of 24 affiliated offices through which unaccompanied refugee minors are placed into foster care, a program administered and funded by HHS/ORR.

Using R&P funds from PRM supplemented by cash and in-kind contributions from private and other sources, the participating agencies provide the following services, consistent with the terms of the R&P cooperative agreement:

- Sponsorship;
- Pre-arrival resettlement planning, including placement;
- Reception on arrival;
- Basic needs support (including housing, furnishings, food, and clothing) for at least 30 days;
- Cultural orientation;
- Assistance with access to health, employment, education, and other services as needed; and
- Development and implementation of an initial resettlement plan for each refugee for 30-90 days.

Office of Refugee Resettlement (ORR)

Through the Refugee Act, Congress directed HHS/ORR to provide refugees with: employment training, English language training, cash assistance (in a manner that promotes independence), and job placement − including providing women with equal opportunities to employment as men − so that refugees can achieve economic self-sufficiency as quickly as possible. ORR is committed to helping refugees transition into the U.S. by providing this assistance and other benefits, services, and guidance that will enable them to achieve self-sufficiency and become integrated members of society. To this end, ORR administers numerous programs, some of which are highlighted below.

State-Administered or Wilson-Fish Programs

Under ORR's state-administered or Wilson-Fish (WF) programs, refugees (who are not eligible for TANF or Medicaid) are eligible to receive up to eight months of *Refugee Cash Assistance (RCA)* and *Refugee Medical Assistance (RMA)* upon arrival. RCA benefits are equivalent to welfare cash benefit levels established by state governments.

The WF program is an alternative to the state-administered program, and is usually administered by local voluntary resettlement agencies. The WF program emphasizes early employment and economic self-sufficiency by integrating cash assistance, case management, and employment services, and by incorporating innovative strategies for the provision of cash assistance (e.g. financial bonuses for early employment). There are currently 13 WF programs nationwide.

ORR also provides states/WF programs with *Formula Refugee Social Services (RSS)* and *Targeted Assistance (TAG)* funds. ORR distributes these funds based on arrival numbers and refugee concentration levels in counties with a high utilization of public assistance. Funding is time limited, and refugees can only access RSS and TAG services up to five years after arrival. These services include: employability services, employment assessment services, on-the-job training, English language instruction, vocational training, case management, translation/interpreter services, social adjustment services, health-related services, home management, and if necessary for employment, day care and transportation.

Additionally, to assist specific groups of refugees, ORR administers the following specialized programs through states/WF programs, including Cuban-Haitian, Older Refugees, Preventive Health, Refugee School Impact, and Targeted Assistance.

Matching Grant Program

The Matching Grant program (MG) is provided through the nine national voluntary agencies that provide R & P services and their resettlement affiliates in 42 states. The objective of MG is to guide refugee households toward economic self-sufficiency through employment within four to six months (120 to 180 days) of program eligibility (usually within the first month of arrival). In MG, self-sufficiency is defined as total household income from employment that enables a family unit to support itself without receipt of public cash assistance. ORR awards $2,200 on a per capita basis to each national voluntary agency, which then allocates funds to its local service providers based on projected enrollments. Agencies provide a 50% match to every federal dollar.

Local service providers ensure core maintenance services for a minimum of 120 days which include housing, transportation, food, and a cash allowance. Clients also receive intensive case management and employment services. Refugees who are unable to attain self-sufficiency by day 120 or 180, may access RCA for the remainder of the eight month eligibility period. In FY 12, over 35,000 individuals were enrolled in the program, 71% of whom achieved self-sufficiency.

Refugee Health

ORR recently created a Division of Refugee Health (DRH) to address the health and well-being of refugees. DRH is working on various initiatives including: collaborating with partners in the implementation of the Affordable Care Act (ACA); administering the Survivors of Torture program; providing technical assistance on medical screening guidelines, mental health awareness and linkages, suicide prevention, emergency preparedness and other health and mental health initiatives (e.g. vision care, autism, etc).

Unaccompanied Refugee Minor (URM) Program

ORR provides funds to 15 states who administer over 20 URM programs. States contract with local licensed foster care agencies that provide specialized placements and services. URMs live in various placements including: traditional and therapeutic foster homes, relatives' homes, group homes, semi-independent and independent living and residential treatment centers. URMs receive various services including: English language training, educational and vocational training, cultural preservation, social integration, family tracing, permanency planning, independent living, and health/mental health care. ORR regulations require states to provide services in parity with the state's Title IV-B foster care plan.

Other Refugee Service Programs

ORR also provides funding to non-profit agencies to focus on special initiatives or programs for refugees including: case management, ethnic community development, home-based child care business development, individual development accounts, microenterprise development, and agricultural projects.

Technical Assistance

ORR provides technical assistance (TA) to resettlement stakeholders through various organizations that have expertise in certain fields. Currently ORR's TA providers assist stakeholders in the areas of community engagement/integration, child welfare, employment, health, Lesbian Gay Bisexual and Transgender (LGBT) populations, survivors of torture, and Temporary Assistance to Needy Families state programs.

III. REGIONAL PROGRAMS

Table 2. Proposed FY 2014 Regional Ceilings by Priority

AFRICA	
Priority 1 Individual Referrals	11,000
Priority 2 Groups	2,500
Priority 3 Family Reunification Refugees	500
Total Proposed:	14,000
EAST ASIA	
Priority 1 Individual Referrals	3,000
Priority 2 Groups	10,800
Priority 3 Family Reunification Refugees	200
Total Proposed:	14,000
EUROPE /CENTRAL ASIA	
Priority 1 Individual Referrals	
Priority 2 Groups	1,000
Priority 3 Family Reunification Refugees	
Total Proposed:	1,000
LATIN AMERICA /CARIBBEAN	
Priority 1 Individual Referrals	400
Priority 2 Groups	4,550
Priority 3 Family Reunification Refugees	50
Total Proposed:	5,000
NEAR EAST /SOUTH ASIA	
Priority 1 Individual Referrals	16,950

Table 2. (Continued)

NEAR EAST /SOUTH ASIA	
Priority 2 Groups	17,000
Priority 3 Family Reunification Refugees	50
Total Proposed:	34,000
UNALLOCATED RESERVE	2,000
TOTAL PROPOSED CEILING:	70,000

Africa

There are currently some 3.2 million refugees across the African continent, constituting roughly 20 percent of the global refugee population. UN-organized repatriations were still underway in 2013 for refugees able to return to safe areas in northwestern Democratic Republic of Congo (DRC), and South Sudan. Organized repatriations to Angola, Liberia, and Rwanda have largely been completed, but residual refugee populations remain. UNHCR recommended cessation of prima facie refugee status for refugees from Angola and Liberia effective June 30, 2012, and for pre-1999 caseload Rwandan refugees effective June 30, 2013. Efforts continue to repatriate those who still wish to return and to locally integrate residual populations where asylum countries agree to provide permanent residence or citizenship.

While there has been significant voluntary repatriation among African refugee populations over the past decade, ongoing conflict in the DRC, Mali, Somalia, and Sudan, and political repression in Eritrea have resulted in over 900,000 new refugees in 2011-2013. Conflict between the Sudanese government and rebel groups has resulted in some 233,000 new Sudanese refugees in South Sudan, Ethiopia, and Kenya since June 2011. In Central African Republic, the Séléka alliance's advance on Bangui caused 49,000 refugees to flee to neighboring countries at the end of 2012 and beginning of 2013, bringing the total number of Central African refugees to over 200,000. Continued fighting and food insecurity in Somalia forced some 67,000 to flee to neighboring countries in the Horn of Africa region in 2012 and over 11,000 to date in 2013, bringing total Somali refugee numbers to over one million. Intensified conflict in eastern DRC has led an additional 110,000 Congolese to seek asylum in Uganda, Rwanda, Burundi, and Zambia since mid-2012. Fighting erupted in northern Mali in January 2012, thus far generating more than 175,000 refugees. Finally, Eritreans continue to seek asylum in neighboring countries due to increasing political repression and the excessive demands of national service; an average of 1,600 in March and April 2013 arrived in Ethiopia (a significant uptick compared to previous average of 800-1,000 per month) and fewer in Sudan, many attempting dangerous onward migration to Europe and the Middle East in search of refuge in countries with better economic opportunities. Conflicts in neighboring regions have also impacted Africa, with the ongoing crisis in Syria resulting in outflows of refugees to Egypt (56,000 registered refugees as of May 28, 2013) and greater North Africa (11,455 registered refugees as of May 2013).

Most African countries honor the principle of first asylum, and for those countries that lack formal mechanisms for asylum, we continue to advocate for the establishment of systems. Traditionally, refugees in Africa have been allowed to remain – and in many cases to effectively economically and/or socially integrate – until voluntary repatriation is possible. However, in most cases, this de facto integration does not include legal integration, such as the granting of legal permanent residence, the right to work, or voting rights. Several countries, including Zambia, Côte d'Ivoire, The Gambia, Ghana, Guinea, Liberia, Nigeria, and Sierra Leone have initiated programs legalizing the status (de jure local integration) of long-staying refugee populations interested in remaining on their territories. In 2008, Tanzania announced a plan to grant citizenship to Burundi refugees who fled their country in 1972. Some 165,000 have accepted the offer of "naturalization," but most do not have official documentation of their new citizenship. Lack of international support for the installation of the "newly naturalized Tanzanians" in new communities could put full implementation in jeopardy.

Religious Freedom

In Sub-Saharan Africa, people are generally free to practice their chosen religions. Governments regularly provide for and respect freedom of religion, although in some countries, such as Eritrea and Sudan, religious freedom is limited, particularly in the midst of ethnic and other conflicts.

The Government of Eritrea is responsible for severe religious freedom abuses in Africa. In recent years the country has engaged in serious religious repression by harassing, arresting, and detaining members of independent evangelical groups, including Pentecostals and Jehovah's Witnesses (who lost certain rights of citizenship for not participating in the 1993 national referendum). Detainees are held in harsh conditions and some have died in custody. The government has also sought greater control over the four State-approved religious groups: the Eritrean Orthodox Church, the Roman Catholic

Church, the Evangelical (Lutheran) Church, and the Islamic community. The government reportedly holds individuals who are jailed for their religious affiliation at various locations. Often detainees are not formally charged, accorded due process, or allowed access to their families. While many are ostensibly jailed for evasion of military conscription, significant numbers were being held solely for their religious beliefs; the current estimate is 1,500 individuals detained on religious grounds. As of December 2012, Human Rights Watch reported that 56 known Jehovah's Witnesses were in detention without access to legal representation, and many had not been charged with a crime. At least three Jehovah's Witnesses had been detained for 15 years, reportedly for evading compulsory military service, a term far beyond the maximum legal penalty of two years for refusing to perform national service.

In Sudan, the government continues to place restrictions on Christians in a manner that is inconsistent with its obligation to uphold freedom of religion. Although there is no penalty for converting from another religion to Islam, converting from Islam is punishable by death. There is no evidence that the current government has ever imposed this penalty, but authorities express their strong prejudice against conversion by occasionally subjecting converts to intense scrutiny, ostracism, and intimidation, or by encouraging converts to leave the country.

Both Eritrea and Sudan are currently designated as "Countries of Particular Concern" (CPC) for particularly severe violations of religious freedom by the Department of State under the International Religious Freedom Act of 1998. The USRAP continues to be available through Priority 1 referrals to Sudanese, Eritrean, and other refugees who are victims of religious intolerance. Refugees from Eritrea and Sudan with certain refugee or asylee family members in the United States will have access to the USRAP through Priority 3. Certain Eritrean refugees in Ethiopia may have access to the USRAP through Priority 2.

In Somalia, a provisional federal constitution replaced the Transitional Federal Charter (TFC) on August 1, 2012. In September, a new parliament elected a new president and ended nearly eight years of transitional governance. The provisional constitution provides for freedom of religion, although it enshrines Islam as the state religion and prohibits proselytism for any religion other than Islam. The trend in the Transitional Federal Government's (TFG) and the new government's respect for freedom of religion did not change significantly during the year. The TFG had limited capacity to enforce the TFC and the new government had limited capacity to enforce the provisional constitution. In addition, the country was fragmented into regions administered by different entities, and neither the TFG nor the new government could implement the TFC or the provisional constitution in areas of the country outside its control. There have also been reports that non-Muslim individuals experience discrimination, violence, and detention because of their religious beliefs. Refugees from Somalia with certain refugee or asylee family members in the United States also have access to the USRAP through Priority 3.

Voluntary Repatriation

Despite the continued existence of protracted refugee situations, voluntary repatriation to improved conditions in the home country remains the most common and desirable durable solution. With the conclusion of various peace agreements and the support of the U.S. Government and other donors, UNHCR has made great progress in promoting and supporting refugee repatriation and reintegration in Africa. Over the past 20 years, net refugee numbers in Africa have fallen by nearly half (from six million at their height in the 1990s to 3.2 million today) even in the face of new outflows.

In West Africa, UNHCR launched its official repatriation program in February 2012 for some 69,000 remaining refugees from Côte d'Ivoire who had fled to Liberia in 2010 and 2011, returning an estimated 12,000 since the program began, though some of these returns were offset by new refugee outflows in 2012. Another 150,000 Ivoirian refugees spontaneously returned home starting in late 2011 following the cessation of post-election hostilities in Côte d'Ivoire. The final round of UNHCR's Liberian repatriation program was completed at the end of December 2012, with more than 155,000 Liberians benefiting from assisted returns since 2004; in all, more than 700,000 Liberians have returned home either spontaneously or with UNHCR assistance. UNHCR continues to focus on facilitating local integration for some 30,000 Liberians who remain in various West African countries – an effort it expects to last through 2013.

In East Africa, the repatriation to South Sudan that started in 2005 was largely concluded in 2011 with the return of more than 370,000 refugees – over 80 percent of the original refugee population of 500,000 has returned. However, due to instability in South Sudan, the pace of returns slowed considerably in 2012. Approximately 117,000 South Sudanese refugees are currently in neighboring countries, including 66,000 who fled the earlier civil war and 51,000 who fled recent fighting in 2012 and 2013. No repatriation initiatives are currently anticipated for the Darfur region of Sudan or Somalia, where insecurity continues to prevent safe and dignified return. Over one million Somalis have sought asylum in neighboring countries, most without any near-term prospect of return to Somalia. Coordination and regional plans for refugee returns when conditions are appropriate in Somalia by host governments (namely Kenya and Ethiopia), the newly-recognized Somali government, and UNHCR are strongly encouraged. Despite the efforts of some asylum countries to repatriate Eritrean refugees, UNHCR has strongly discouraged returns to Eritrea given ongoing political repression and harsh treatment of returnees.

In Central Africa, most organized repatriation to Burundi ended in 2010 and there have been over 500,000 returns since 2002, including over 53,000 of the 1972-caseload refugees who chose not to accept the Government of Tanzania's offer of naturalization. Repatriation of the last of the 1993-era Burundi refugees in Tanzania was completed with the closure of Mtabila Camp in December 2012. Although the majority of Rwandan refugees returned home in the late 1990's, some 50,000-100,000 remain in exile. With the invocation of the cessation clause for pre-1999 Rwandan refugees on June 30, 2013, remaining Rwandans may be required either to repatriate or to seek other means of remaining in asylum countries. Repatriation to relatively stable areas of eastern DRC wound down in 2011 with the conclusion of returns from Zambia and Tanzania to the Katanga Province, but renewed hostilities between the GDRC and the M23 rebel group erased most of these gains and North and South Kivu provinces remain mostly too insecure for large-scale refugee return and, in fact, have been characterized by significant new internal displacement and new refugee flows. Ethnic violence that erupted in late 2009 in Equateur Province forced some 160,000 Congolese to flee to the Central African Republic (CAR) and the Republic of Congo. A facilitated repatriation began in May 2012, and, as of May 2013, more than 72,000 refugees have been repatriated back to northwestern DRC. UNHCR hopes to repatriate an additional 15,000 refugees by the end of 2013. Additionally, the persistent threat of attack posed by the Lord's Resistance Army (LRA) in northeastern DRC, southeastern CAR, and South Sudan continues to cause instability in the region, preventing the return of some 40,000 refugees and 400,000 IDPs displaced by the LRA since 2008.

Local Integration

In a number of protracted situations, refugees have been able to become self-sufficient, and their camps and settlements have been efficiently integrated both economically and socially into the host communities, even as legal rights lag behind. This integration dynamic has occurred particularly for refugees who fled during the 1960s through the early 1980s to countries that had arable land available, allowing many refugees to move out of camps. Despite such de facto integration, refugees residing among the local population did not necessarily enjoy the rights, entitlements, or economic opportunities available to legal residents. As a result, this piecemeal integration was often an interim, rather than a durable, solution for many African refugees.

More recently, however, a number of African countries have offered more formal integration as a durable solution for residual refugee populations who will not or cannot repatriate. In conjunction with UNHCR, the Governments of Côte d'Ivoire, The Gambia, Ghana, Guinea, Liberia, Nigeria, and Sierra Leone launched a regional local integration program for Liberian and Sierra Leonean refugees in 2007. That program provided refugees opportunities for economic self-reliance; activities to enhance the quality of their social integration; and legal rights and documentation, including access to citizenship in some countries and freedom of movement in all countries under the protocols of the Economic Community of West African States (ECOWAS). The Government of Zambia has pledged to provide permanent residence status to 10,000 former Angolan refugees – mainly refugees who arrived before 1986, were born in Zambia, or are married to Zambians -- and is currently reviewing applications for those who meet eligibility criteria.

Senegal offered Mauritanian refugees who wished to remain in Senegal the option of becoming Senegalese citizens in 2007, and UNHCR, in partnership with the Senegalese government, launched a campaign in 2012 to provide digitized and biometric identity cards to some 19,000 refugees (of whom 14,000 were Mauritanians) by the end of the year. The card guarantees holders the same rights as Senegalese citizens, including the right to residence in the country and to travel to ECOWAS member states. The Governments of Uganda and Mozambique have previously stated their intention to provide refugees with local integration opportunities and citizenship, but have not yet passed the required legislation. As mentioned above, the Government of Tanzania offered to provide permanent settlement and citizenship to nearly 200,000 1972-era Burundi refugees; some 165,000 accepted the offer and were collectively naturalized, although the vast majority have not yet received documentation and the modalities of the integration process are still being negotiated. While not formal integration programs, a few countries have permitted refugees to live where they choose, outside of camps (Uganda and Niger, for example) or have temporarily adapted to natural rural to urban migration that involves refugees as well as nationals (for example, Kenya until late 2012), Ethiopia formally introduced an out-of-camp policy for Eritrean refugees in August 2010, allowing Eritreans to live outside camps if they are able to support themselves or if they have someone to sponsor them financially. While it does not give Eritrean refugees the right to work, it does offer additional educational opportunities, including tertiary education.

Third-Country Resettlement

Given the political and economic volatility in many parts of Africa, resettlement to third countries outside the region is an essential durable solution and element of protection for certain refugees. With limited opportunities for permanent integration in many countries of asylum and the protracted nature of some refugee situations, the need for third-country resettlement of African refugees is expected to continue despite the overall decrease in the refugee population on the continent. In recent years, UNHCR has increasingly viewed resettlement as an important tool of protection for refugees in Africa and has shown an increase in resettlement referrals this past year. Several resettlement countries – including Canada and Australia – accept significant numbers of African refugees, but the United States resettles far more than any other country.

FY 2013 U.S. Admissions

We project nearly 15,000 African refugee arrivals in FY 2013 – higher than the anticipated number at the beginning of the year, thanks largely to progress made in clearing security checks more quickly.

Four countries of origin (Somalia, DRC, Eritrea, and Sudan) currently account for the vast majority of U.S. admissions from the region. In East Africa, we continue to process P-1 Somalis in Kakuma refugee camp. Although processing in Dadaab camp has been suspended since October 2011 due to the security situation there, PRM funded the construction of a transit center in Kakuma to house refugees from Dadaab who were still awaiting interview. PRM moved approximately 1,700 refugees from Dadaab to Kakuma in FY 2013 for adjudication and out-processing. We admitted more refugees out of Ethiopia than from any other country in Africa this year, primarily Somalis from camps in the east and Eritreans from the northern camps, with approximately 3,500 departures to the United States. We are also processing an increasing number of DRC Congolese from Rwanda as part of the effort by UNHCR to refer 50,000 DRC Congolese for resettlement from Rwanda, Uganda, Tanzania and Burundi over the next 5-7 years.

For the West Africa region, we continue to interview refugees from the Central African Republic in Southern Chad. We have completed the processing of the residual P-3 Liberian and Sierra Leonean caseloads in West Africa and will not take any new applications. This completion was made in time for the re-start of the P-3 family reunification program of the USRAP which launched at the start of FY 2013.

We expect to see approximately 1,500 refugees admitted from the Southern Africa region, mainly Somalis from South Africa and DRC Congolese from elsewhere in the region; and just over 500 refugee admissions from West Africa mainly consisting of Central Africans processed in Chad. In all, we expect to admit refugees of more than 24 African nationalities, processed in 32 countries during FY 2013.

FY 2014 U.S. Resettlement Program

We propose up to 14,000 resettlement numbers for African refugees in FY 2014. PRM has actively engaged relevant offices within the Department of State, UNHCR, the NGO community, and DHS/USCIS to identify caseloads appropriate for resettlement consideration. As a result of these discussions, PRM has identified a number of nationalities and groups for priority processing during FY 2014.

From East and Southern Africa, we expect 11,000-12,000 admissions, primarily Somalis in Ethiopia, Kenya, Djibouti, and South Africa; Eritreans in Ethiopia and in Sudan; Congolese from Rwanda and Uganda, and additional small numbers of P-1 referrals of various nationalities in the countries above, as well as in Namibia, Zambia, and Zimbabwe. This number includes individuals who are referred based on a P-2 designation in Rwanda: survivors of a series of massacres that took place at the Mudende transit camp in Rwanda in 1997. We are also expecting UNHCR to refer approximately 200 unaccompanied refugee minors from camps in northern Ethiopia. From West and Central Africa, we expect some 500 admissions. We anticipate a steady stream of referrals of Central African Republic refugees in Southern Chad, and we also intend to re-start the resettlement program for Sudanese Darfuris in Eastern Chad. UNHCR has referred some 1,000 individuals in Eastern Chad that will be processed in FY 2014.

Outside of sub-Saharan Africa, we anticipate up to 2,000 Sudanese, Somali, Ethiopian, Eritrean and other sub-Saharan African refugees to be processed in Tunisia, Egypt, Lebanon, Turkey, Jordan and Russia. Processing in these locations largely depends on the local security situation which will determine if teams of DHS/USCIS refugee officers can access these locations.

Proposed FY 2014 Africa Program to Include Arrivals from the Following Categories

Priority 1 Individual Referrals	11,000
Priority 2 Groups	2,500
Priority 3 Family Reunification	500
Total Proposed Ceiling	14,000

East Asia

Several East Asian countries host large and diverse refugee populations. Recent years have seen important developments for these groups, particularly involving the strategic use of resettlement as a durable solution. Thailand, Malaysia, Bangladesh, and India continue to host large numbers of Burmese refugees and asylum-seekers. The U.S. Government continues to press for meaningful political and democratic reform and national reconciliation with ethnic minority groups in Burma, while recognizing reforms made over the past year by easing financial and investment sanctions. The international community continues to engage in discussions regarding the voluntary return of Burmese refugees, but acknowledges that ongoing conflict and the long road towards peace, national reconciliation and development make large-scale return of refugees in safety and with dignity a longer-term goal.

The resettlement of more than 100,000 Burmese refugees from Thailand since 2006 – including more than 68,000 to the United States – has significantly reduced the number of Burmese refugees in the camps who are eligible for the U.S. P-2 resettlement program. After more than seven years of large-scale resettlement, we are approaching the natural conclusion of the group resettlement program that has specific eligibility criteria for Burmese refugees who were re-registered by UNHCR in 2005 and formally registered by the Government of Thailand. In January 2013, we began making rolling announcement deadlines for eligible Burmese refugees to apply for U.S. resettlement that vary by camp based on when resettlement operations began. So far, rolling announcements have been made in six of the nine camps, with the final three likely to be completed by the end of 2013. The P-2 resettlement program will continue until we have completed the processing of every application received by the deadline for each camp. Refugees are not being asked to make a decision about returning to Burma but instead, the smaller numbers of refugees who are eligible for resettlement are being asked to decide if they want to pursue this opportunity. Those who do not exercise this option will be able to remain in the camps until safe and voluntary returns are possible. The United States will continue to accept individual referrals from UNHCR for all nationalities.

Since 2006, UNHCR Malaysia has operated the second largest refugee status determination program in the world. As of April 2013, there were 102,070 persons of concern registered with UNHCR in Malaysia of which 93,600, or 92 percent, are from Burma (32,360 Chin, 26,910 stateless Rohingya from Burma's Northern Rakhine State, 7,210 Rakhines, 10,540 Burmese Muslims, 3,590 Mon, 12,990 Kachins and other ethnic minorities). In addition, some 8,460 asylum-seekers and refugees from various countries – primarily Afghanistan, Iraq, Somalia, and Sri Lanka – are registered with UNHCR in Malaysia. Malaysia is not a party to the 1951 Convention relating to the Status of Refugees or its 1967 Protocol. We support UNHCR's efforts to use resettlement as a strategic tool to assist refugees in Malaysia.

In July 1991, more than 250,000 Burmese Rohingya suffering de jure statelessness and oppression due to their Muslim faith and ethnicity migrated from northern Rakhine State to Bangladesh. During the 1990s, over 230,000 Rohingya refugees were voluntarily repatriated from Bangladesh, leaving behind nearly 30,000 refugees, who remain in two official refugee camps in southeastern Bangladesh. An additional 9,000 unregistered Rohingya reside in an unofficial settlement in Leda and approximately 26,000 unregistered Rohingya reside in the makeshift Kutupalong camp. In addition, an unknown number who had previously repatriated, have again returned to Bangladesh and are now living without UNHCR protection. Anywhere between 200,000-500,000 unregistered Rohingya live outside of the two official UNHCR refugee camps in the Cox's Bazaar district. UNHCR continues to work to enhance protection and address security concerns caused by growing tensions between both registered refugees and unregistered Rohingya and local Bangladeshis living outside of the camps.

The cases of more than 500 individual Rohingyas, including 281 individuals approved for resettlement to several countries, have been on hold since October 2010 when the Government of Bangladesh (GOB) halted resettlement activities pending a review of their refugee policy; the GOB has yet to issue a formal decision on a national refugee policy. We are prepared to resume resettlement activity immediately following a GOB decision. In addition, we expect ongoing UNHCR referrals of urban Burmese in India.

As reflected in the North Korean Human Rights Act, the United States remains deeply concerned about the human rights situation of North Koreans both inside the Democratic People's Republic of Korea and in various countries in the region. The United States began resettling interested, eligible North Korean refugees in 2006 and remains committed to continuing this program.

Religious Freedom

Although many governments in East Asia do not restrict religious freedom, religious believers face serious persecution in several countries. The DPRK, China, and Burma are designated by the Department of State as CPCs under the International Religious Freedom Act of 1998 for systematic, ongoing, and egregious violations of religious freedom.

The DPRK severely restricts religious freedom, including organized religious activity, except that which is supervised tightly by officially recognized groups linked to the government. Although the DPRK constitution provides for "freedom of religious belief," genuine religious freedom does not exist. Little is known about the day-to-day life of religious persons in the country. Religious and human rights groups outside of the country have provided numerous reports that members of underground churches have been beaten, arrested, tortured, or killed because of their religious beliefs.

While the constitutions of China, Burma, and Vietnam provide for freedom of religion, in practice, these governments restrict or repress religious activities of some members of religious communities in a manner that is inconsistent with their commitments to uphold freedom of religion.

The Chinese government continues to harass and interfere with unregistered religious groups, most notably the unofficial Catholic churches loyal to the Holy See, Protestant "house churches," some Muslim groups (especially ethnic Uighur Muslims in Xinjiang Uighur Autonomous Region), members of the Falun Gong, and Tibetan Buddhists loyal to the Dalai Lama. Certain religious or spiritual groups are banned by law. The criminal law defines banned groups as "evil cults" and those belonging to them can be sentenced to prison. This includes Falun Gong and some other qigong-based groups, in addition to some Christian groups. Religious believers have been harassed, arrested, detained in "black jails" without due process, sent to forced labor camps, and sentenced to long jail terms. There have been credible allegations of torture.

In Burma, the government continues to discriminate against religious minorities, in particular stateless Rohingya Muslims.

Vietnam and the United States signed an agreement on religious freedom in May 2005, under which Vietnam committed to improving the status of religious freedom in Vietnam. As a result of the progress Vietnam made after signing the agreement, the U.S. Government removed Vietnam from the CPC list in November 2006. Over the past three years, Vietnam's religious freedom record has been mixed. Progress has been made with regard to the registration/recognition of religious groups and congregations. In addition, religious groups have experienced expanded freedom of assembly. However, there are also reports of harassment at the local level, including through the use of land laws. Several Protestant congregations in rural areas continue to report harassment, including beatings and forced renunciations.

Nationals of the DPRK, Vietnam, China, Laos, and Burma have access to the U.S. Refugee Admissions Program. North Korean and Burmese refugees also have access to family reunification processing through Priority 3.

Voluntary Repatriation

Although the Burmese government has taken steps to implement some democratic and political reforms, ongoing fighting continues between the Burmese Army and ethnic minority groups in Kachin and Shan States. National peace and reconciliation efforts will take time; thus, the repatriation of most Burmese refugees in Thailand, Bangladesh, Malaysia, India and elsewhere is not currently a viable solution.

Local Integration

Due to fears of a "pull factor," countries in the region have traditionally been reluctant to integrate refugees or to grant asylum. We hope that U.S. efforts to resettle large numbers of refugees from the camps along the Thai-Burma border will encourage the Thai government to improve livelihood opportunities for those refugees who will not be resettled. The United States and other donor governments continue to engage in a strategic dialogue with the Royal Thai government concerning the future of the nine camps on the Thai-Burma border. We recognize that the Thai government remains concerned that resettlement has not dramatically reduced the camp population as a mixture of new arrivals and Burmese who were living just outside of the camps are taking the place of those who are departing for third countries. Local integration remains a difficult option, due to opposition from host countries, such as Thailand, Bangladesh, Malaysia, and India. UNHCR and the international community continue to advocate for these governments to make policy changes relating to refugees, and to expand humanitarian protection and assistance space for refugees and other persons of concern.

Third-Country Resettlement

The United States continues to lead third country resettlement efforts in the region. Other resettlement countries, including Australia, Canada, New Zealand, and the Nordic countries, resettle refugees referred by UNHCR. In FY 2013, the United States processed UNHCR-referred refugee cases in China, the Hong Kong Special Administrative Region, Indonesia, Malaysia, the Republic of Korea, Thailand, and Vietnam.

FY 2013 U.S. Admissions

We expect to admit up to 17,000 refugees from East Asia in FY 2013. This will include up to 8,000 Burmese ethnic minorities (mostly Karen, Karenni, and Kachin) living in camps along the Thai-Burma border, some 9,000 Burmese (of various ethnic minorities) in Malaysia, and a small number of urban refugees of various nationalities in the region.

FY 2014 U.S. Resettlement Program

We expect to admit up to 14,000 refugees from East Asia in FY 2014. This will include up to 5,000 Burmese ethnic minorities (mostly Karen and Karenni) living in camps along the Thai-Burma border, some 9,000 Burmese (of various ethnic minorities) in Malaysia, and a small number of urban refugees of various nationalities in the region.

Proposed FY 2014 East Asia Program to Include Arrivals from the Following Categories

Priority 1 Individual Referrals	3,000
Priority 2 Groups	10,800
Priority 3 Family Reunification	200
Total Proposed Ceiling	14,000

Europe and Central Asia

Europe continues to host large refugee populations, as well as other persons affected by conflict, who, over the last two decades, have been left in situations of protracted displacement – often in dire conditions. In its 2012-2013 Global Appeal, UNHCR reported that there were nearly 4.4 million asylum seekers, refugees, internally displaced persons, stateless individuals, or other persons "of concern" throughout Europe and Central Asia. Many had fled conflicts outside the region, such as in Afghanistan and Syria, but the estimates also include persons claiming persecution within Eurasia, including hundreds of thousands of refugees and IDPs in the Balkans.

With the 2012 accession of Bulgaria, Portugal and the Republic of Moldova to the 1954 and 1961 Statelessness Conventions, and Hungary's decision to lift its reservations to the 1954 Convention, 36 of the 49 States in Europe are now party to the 1954 Convention. Twenty-four are party to the 1961 Convention. All countries of the Russian Federation and Central Asia except Uzbekistan have acceded to the 1951 Convention relating to the Status of Refugees and its 1967 Protocol. However, compliance with these instruments remains problematic. Despite sustained efforts by UNHCR and other stakeholders to build protection capacity and help strengthen asylum systems and protection laws in the region, results have been modest, thus far. Many of these countries have been slow or reluctant to recognize and integrate refugees and other at-risk individuals. The protection provided by some regional governments to refugees, asylum seekers, and other migrants is limited and public intolerance, including attacks against non-Slavic foreigners, is common. There are documented cases of refoulement. UNHCR has been working with many of these governments to establish and/or reform asylum procedures and refugee protection laws.

The 1990's break-up of the Soviet Union also created newly independent states with sizeable populations of stateless individuals due to gaps in nationality laws and inconsistent implementation of those laws. Difficulty in establishing citizenship at the time of succession has also created later problems for children born to an undocumented parent(s). The problem of statelessness remains in the region, although some states, such as Turkmenistan, have taken steps to register stateless individuals and facilitate their acquisition of nationality.

According to UNHCR, at the end of 2012, there were approximately 440,000 refugees and IDPs in the Balkans, almost all of whom have been displaced for a decade or longer. An estimated 210,000 persons of this population are displaced from Kosovo, most of whom are currently living in Serbia. It is estimated that 97,000 individuals in this group are in need of assistance. Since 2000, the overall level of return to Kosovo from Serbia has been low. There have been over 23,000 voluntary returns of minorities to Kosovo since the conflict ended. Housing, documentation issues, a lack of employment opportunity, and occasional violence directed against ethnic Serbs in Kosovo has limited return prospects.

From 2010 to 2012, the countries of the region – with the assistance of the international community – made significant progress toward resolving a large part of the refugee situation in the Balkans. A November 2011 ministerial meeting in Belgrade brought together Ministers of Foreign Affairs from Serbia, Croatia, Bosnia and Herzegovina and Montenegro to sign a Joint Declaration expressing their collective will to resolve the protracted refugee and displacement situation, and they committed their countries to a Regional Housing Program (RHP) for refugees and IDPs supported by international donors. The RHP was designed to create durable solutions for 74,000 of the most vulnerable refugees in those countries. While principally affecting housing, the RHP has established the Regional Coordination Forum to discuss other pertinent issues such as pensions, civil documentation, exchange of data and other public information. A donors' conference in April 2012 succeeded in raising over $340 million (€260 million) in international funds to support the RHP over five years. The United States provided $10 million in FY 2012, and U.S. involvement is seen as a critical ingredient to the RHP's success.

Religious Freedom

The status of religious freedom varies widely across Europe and Central Asia. Among the various states in this region, some mandate the registration of religious groups. Nontraditional religious groups are sometimes labeled as "sects" or "cults" by their home governments and may be subject to special scrutiny and limited privileges. Registration typically carries the right to rent or own property, hold religious services, appoint military and prison chaplains, and receive state subsidies. Restitution of religious properties is an issue yet to be fully resolved. Uzbekistan is designated by the Department of State as a CPC under the International Religious Freedom Act of 1998 for systematic, ongoing, and egregious violations of religious freedom.

Manifestations of anti-Semitism continue throughout the region, including demonstrations by extremist groups, physical and verbal assaults, and vandalism of cemeteries, synagogues, and monuments; in several countries, openly anti-Semitic political parties have gained seats in parliament. Government officials and elected members of parliaments have also been responsible for anti-Semitic statements and acts. While most incidents have taken place in former communist bloc countries, a number of western European countries have faced a disturbing increase in anti-Semitism, in addition to anti-Muslim sentiment.

The Russian government uses its anti-extremism law to justify raids, arrests, and bans on religious literature of peaceful, "non-traditional" minority religious groups, including readers of Muslim theologian Said Nursi, Jehovah's Witnesses, Scientologists, Falun Gong practitioners, and some Protestant groups.

In Turkey, some religious minority communities face difficulties owning property, registering places of worship, training clergy, and obtaining visas for religious workers. Conscientious objectors on the basis of their faith are sometimes arrested and prosecuted for failing to comply with laws mandating military service, as previously witnessed in Armenia, Azerbaijan, Belarus, Turkey, and Turkmenistan.

Muslims across Europe and Central Asia have sometimes been viewed as potential threats and accused of membership in internationally banned groups. In some countries, there are legal restrictions or prohibitions on the wearing of religious attire in schools and in public.

Restrictions on religious freedom in Central Asia are often justified in the name of maintaining stability and combating terrorism. Some governments believe that religious freedom will result in competing centers of power and influence or open the door to violent extremism, although research shows that government suppression often results in increased violence and loss of regime legitimacy. Non-violent, non-extremist religious minorities such as the Jehovah's Witnesses and Nursi readers, are often targets, as well as majorities from dominant religions that may include new streams of belief.

Since 1989, the USRAP has offered resettlement consideration to individuals from certain religious minorities in the nations that made up the former Soviet Union who also have close family ties to the United States. Under the Lautenberg Amendment, Jews, Evangelical Christians, and certain members of the Ukrainian Catholic or Ukrainian Orthodox Churches are considered under a reduced evidentiary standard when being considered for refugee status. In recent years, fewer new applications and low approval rates have resulted in fewer departures to the United States. Individuals of all nationalities throughout the region may be referred for Priority 1 processing.

Voluntary Repatriation

The international community continues to support efforts to create favorable conditions for the return of ethnic minorities to their homes in the Balkans. In June 2006, Serbian, Kosovo, and UN authorities signed the Protocol on Voluntary and Sustainable Return to Kosovo, which sought to improve the conditions for return by focusing on three elements: ensuring the safety of returnees, returning property to the displaced and rebuilding their houses, and creating an overall environment that sustains returns. There is still much work to be done in ensuring that those hoping to return have all the means to do so. PRM supported the return process through a grant to Mercy Corps in FY 2012 that promoted sustainable return through shelter repair, income-generation activities including vocational training and the provision of agricultural inputs, as well as programming to facilitate inter-ethnic dialogue. International funding continues to facilitate and sustain the return and reintegration of displaced minorities from Kosovo. The Regional Housing program will allow thousands of returns to take place in Serbia, Croatia, Bosnia and Herzegovina, and Montenegro. The program will encourage both voluntary repatriation and local integration as durable solutions.

Local Integration

UNHCR has led efforts to create viable asylum systems and effective legal protections for refugees in the Balkans, the Russian Federation, the South Caucasus and Central Asia. However, ineffective implementation of these laws, combined with the history of national animosities and xenophobia throughout the region, often makes effective local integration difficult for ethnic minority refugees. In Azerbaijan, a majority of refugees lack legal status, despite being recognized by UNHCR and permitted by the government to stay in the country. As such, refugees do not have access to legal employment, making local integration in Azerbaijan extremely difficult. In Russia, difficulties in acquiring citizenship remain for some former Soviet citizens who resided in Russia before 1992 and are, under Russian law, entitled to Russian citizenship. Groups such as the Meskhetian Turks have been unable to obtain Russian citizenship and thus remain de facto stateless. In Russia, UNHCR focuses on quality-assurance measures to strengthen the national asylum system, including access to the asylum system at borders, and to contribute to the Government's plans to bring its reception infrastructure and processes up to full international standards. In Montenegro, the path to citizenship has been particularly slow for those displaced from Kosovo. The Regional Housing Program should provide an easier path to local integration for some of the most vulnerable, including Roma populations, among this group. The Government of Serbia is implementing integration programs for some displaced persons from Kosovo.

Third-Country Resettlement

The United States continues to accept refugees from the region, almost exclusively religious minorities from Russia and Eurasia processed under the

Lautenberg Amendment. Jewish immigration to Israel from the region continues under the United Israel Appeal Program.

FY 2013 U.S. Admissions

In FY 2013 we estimate fewer than 1,000 admissions from Europe and Central Asia. Religious minorities processed under the Lautenberg Amendment from countries of the former Soviet Union constitute nearly the entire caseload. During FY 2012, applicants were processed in Almaty, Baku, Bishkek, Chisinau, Kyiv, Valletta, Minsk, Tbilisi, Moscow, Timisoara, and Tashkent.

FY 2014 U.S. Resettlement Program

The proposed FY 2014 ceiling for refugees from Europe and Central Asia is 1,000 individuals. Priority 2 includes individuals who will be processed under Lautenberg guidelines in the states of the former Soviet Union. Low approval rates for this Priority 2 program and a reduced rate of new applications serve to limit the number of admissions.

Proposed FY 2013 Europe and Central Asia Program to Include Arrivals from the Following Categories

Priority 1 Individual Referrals	0
Priority 2 Groups	1,000
Priority 3 Family Reunification	0
Total Proposed Ceiling	1,000

Latin America and the Caribbean

At the end of 2012, the number of refugees, asylum seekers, IDPs, and other people of concern in Latin America and the Caribbean totaled over 5 million. The ongoing conflict in Colombia generated the largest numbers of refugees and IDPs in the region. Estimates of the number of IDPs in Colombia vary between 4.8 million (government figure) and 5.4 million (NGO figure). Expanded state presence and improved security in cities and towns throughout Colombia led to a decline in internal displacement in 2009 and 2010. However, displacement increased in 2011 as a result of confrontations between the Government of Colombia (GOC) and illegal armed groups, including the Revolutionary Armed Forces of Colombia (FARC), the National

Liberation Army (ELN), criminal gangs (BACRIM) and criminal narco-trafficking networks. The GOC registered 66,634 IDPs in 2012 and expects this figure to increase as declarations continue to be filed and the backlog is addressed. According to UNHCR, it is likely that displacement will continue to grow. In surrounding countries, including Ecuador, Venezuela, Costa Rica, and Panama, there are some 400,000 Colombian asylum seekers, refugees, and persons in refugee-like situations.

The number of Colombian asylum seekers, refugees, and persons of concern in neighboring countries continues to rise. Ecuador has the highest number of recognized Colombian refugees and asylum seekers in Latin America. The Government of Ecuador (GOE) has recognized around 56,000 as refugees and reports that 14,567 are pending refugee status determination (RSD) by the GOE, although UNHCR estimates that the actual figure is nearly triple that. The asylum process in Ecuador is slow and difficult to access, and the refugee approval rate is around seven percent. In May 2012, the GOE issued Presidential Decree 1182, which limited the amount of time that asylum seekers have to file a claim to 15 days, in addition to the pre-admissibility step to the RSD process, which has created additional delays. Asylum seekers pending RSD can wait up to a year for a decision, and now have the right to work in the interim. UNHCR participates in the asylum process but has highlighted a deteriorating protection environment in Ecuador for refugees, citing delays in registration and revocations of refugee status, labor exploitation, a more active presence of illegal armed groups and criminal gangs, forced recruitment of minors, and increasing xenophobia and discrimination. Other countries in the region, such as Costa Rica, Venezuela, the Dominican Republic, and Panama, also have established asylum procedures, but the registration and determination procedures are often implemented ineffectively. UNHCR is working with these countries, including Ecuador, to improve their asylum processes.

In Panama, there are approximately 1,500 recognized refugees (mainly Colombians). In 2011, the Government of Panama passed Law 356 granting over 900 Colombians living in the Darien Province under Temporary Humanitarian Protection (PTH in Spanish) status the ability to apply for permanent residency and work permits. The process of applying for permanent residency has been slow, however, and no residency requests have yet been granted to PTH holders. In Costa Rica, there are approximately 13,000 recognized refugees. Under a new migration law, Costa Rica re-established its Refugee Department in March 2010, along with a Migration Tribunal. Decisions in asylum cases in Costa Rica can take up to a year. There are approximately 4,000 recognized refugees in Venezuela, and UNHCR estimates there are another 200,000 persons living in a refugee-like situation in the country. In Brazil, there are over 4,000 recognized refugees from 75 different countries; the largest numbers are from Angola and Colombia.

Religious Freedom

In Latin America and the Caribbean, religious freedom is widely recognized and supported by government and society, though there are cases of religious intolerance. In some isolated instances, Christian groups, mainly Evangelicals, Protestants, and Mormons have reported impediments or complications to their practice of religion, establishment of religious institutions, and importation of religious materials. In some areas, there is harassment of Muslims, anti-Muslim cartoons and speech, and marginalization of Afro and indigenous religions. In Cuba, significant government restrictions remain in place.

Although the constitution protects religious freedom, the Government of Cuba continued to control most aspects of religious life, including interference in church affairs, surveillance of religious institutions, harassment of outspoken church leaders, and assault of worshipers. The U.S. Refugee Admissions Program in Havana offers Cubans who have been persecuted on a number of grounds, including their religious beliefs, the opportunity for permanent resettlement in the United States. However, the Government of Cuba declined to provide the necessary exit visas to some individuals. We will monitor the implementation of the January 2013 abolition of the exit permit requirement to see if these individuals are still prevented from traveling.

Manifestations of anti-Semitism that occurred throughout the hemisphere at times appeared correlated to the unfolding transitions to democracy in other parts of the world. In Venezuela, anti-Semitism is a growing concern, including instances of anti-Semitism in the government-controlled media.

Voluntary Repatriation

Given the threats and violence in Colombia from illegal armed groups (non-state actors) and the lack of state presence to provide full protection in some areas, UNHCR does not actively promote repatriation of Colombian refugees.

Local Integration

The Governments of Costa Rica, Ecuador, Panama, and Venezuela have maintained policies that theoretically allow Colombians in need of protection to obtain asylum and integrate locally, although the processes involved are usually slow and cumbersome. The governments' capacity to review applications and confer refugee status remains limited. Even registered refugees with the right to work in these countries struggle to find stable employment or income opportunities, competing with the large number of poor in host communities. Colombians seeking international protection face rising levels of discrimination and xenophobia, and the ability to locally integrate in some areas is becoming more difficult. Furthermore, refugees do not live in camps, but rather the large majority live in urban areas. Some Colombian persons of concern (including refugees and asylum seekers) in Ecuador, Costa Rica, and Venezuela continue to experience harassment by persons associated with armed Colombian groups operating in these countries. In recent years, the refugee status determination process in Costa Rica has shown some improvement, but delays in recognition and documentation still exist. For asylum seekers in Panama, the situation is complicated, as the government continues to be reluctant to receive Colombian refugees or confer even minimal protection. Security remains a major concern for the Government of Panama, and Panamanians often equate refugees with drug trafficking and crime.

The Department of State is currently supporting UNHCR's efforts to assist the Dominican Republic and other Caribbean countries in developing systems for conducting refugee status determinations for asylum seekers, including Haitians. The opening of a UNHCR office in the Dominican Republic in 2010 and the agency's continued presence in Haiti have contributed greatly to its ability to address the protection needs of refugees, asylum-seekers, and displaced and stateless persons in mixed migration flows throughout the region. In FY2013, UNHCR undertook a refugee mapping initiative through which the organization captured registration information for 144 refugee households and 203 asylum-seeker households. Despite past delays, the Dominican Republic's refugee eligibility committee (CONARE) met in June 2012. Prior to this meeting, the CONARE had not made a decision on an asylum claim since 2005, and had not made more than 20 decisions since UNHCR handed over responsibility for refugee status determinations to the government in 1997.

Third and in-Country Resettlement

In the past, local integration had been the solution best suited to regional refugee problems in Latin America. In recent years, however, third-country resettlement has become an important alternative for those who face physical risks and have urgent protection needs. Canada, New Zealand, Sweden, Denmark, Norway, and the United States offer resettlement to at-risk Colombian refugees. Currently, the United States accepts referrals from UNHCR and embassies in the region and processes these cases principally in Ecuador and Costa Rica, with occasional cases in other countries throughout the region. Under the "Solidarity Resettlement Program," a component of the Mexico Plan of Action which sought regional solutions to the Colombian refugee issue, countries in the region including Argentina, Brazil, Chile, and Uruguay are working with UNHCR to resettle a modest number of Colombian refugees. As noted earlier, the Department of State is providing technical support to bolster Uruguay's resettlement program. The United States also facilitates the resettlement to third countries of persons interdicted by the U.S. Coast Guard or who enter Guantanamo Naval Station directly and are found by DHS/USCIS to have a well-founded fear of persecution or to be more likely than not to face torture if repatriated to their country of origin. From 1996 to date, approximately 400 such protected persons have been resettled to 20 countries worldwide.

The U.S. Government continues to operate an in-country refugee resettlement program in Cuba. We have taken steps to ensure that all Cubans eligible for consideration have access to the program and that approved refugees travel as soon as possible. The number of persons seeking refugee resettlement remains high and there is a substantial backlog of cases pending review, an unknown number of which are likely ineligible for the program. Additional resources are being applied to address the backlogged cases, and we expect the backlog will continue to decrease by the end of FY2013. Recent upgrades to the Refugee Annex have been completed, thus allowing the Mission to expand the Cultural Orientation program for approved applicants. Unfortunately, the Cuban Government interferes with USRAP's communications with some individuals, causing delays, misunderstandings, or misinformation. Some approved refugees do not have sufficient funds to pay for the medical exams and passports needed to depart Cuba. Although the exit permit requirement was abolished on January 14, 2013, the Cuban government continues to prevent certain Cuban citizens from traveling.

Cubans currently eligible to apply for admission to the United States through the in-country program include the following:

1) Former political prisoners;
2) Members of persecuted religious minorities;
3) Human rights activists;

4) Forced labor conscripts (1965-68);
5) Persons deprived of their professional credentials or subjected to other disproportionately harsh or discriminatory treatment resulting from their perceived or actual political or religious beliefs; and
6) Persons who have experienced or fear harm because of their relationship – family or social – to someone who falls under one of the preceding categories.

FY 2013 U.S. Admissions

We anticipate admitting close to 4,500 refugees from Latin America and the Caribbean during FY 2013. Cubans compose the overwhelming majority of refugees resettled from the region. Historically, most Cuban admissions were former political prisoners and forced labor conscripts. The program was expanded in 1991 to include human rights activists, displaced professionals, and others with claims of persecution, which currently compose the majority of admissions. We expect over 100 Colombian refugees to be admitted to the United States during FY 2013.

FY 2014 U.S. Resettlement Program

The proposed 5,000 ceiling for Latin America and the Caribbean for FY 2014 comprises Cuban refugees eligible for the in-country Priority 2 program; a small number of UNHCR-referred Priority 1 Colombians; as well as a small number of Priority 3 family reunification cases.

Proposed FY 2014 Latin America Program to Include Arrivals from the Following Categories

Priority 1 Individual Referrals	400
Priority 2 (In-Country Cubans)	4,550
Priority 3 Family Reunification	50
Total Proposed Ceiling	5,000

Near East and South Asia

The Near East/South Asia region remains host to millions of refugees, primarily Iraqis, Palestinians, Afghans, Iranians, Tibetans, Sri Lankans, Bhutanese, and now Syrians. Few countries in the region are party to the 1951 Convention relating to the Status of Refugees and/or its 1967 Protocol.

Nonetheless, many host governments tolerate the presence of refugees within their borders.

UNHCR, the International Committee of the Red Cross, IOM, the World Food Program, the United Nations Relief and Works Agency for Palestine Refugees in the Near East, and other humanitarian organizations work with refugees in the region. Some countries have provided long-term protection and/or asylum, mainly to Tibetans, Bhutanese, Sri Lankans, Palestinians, Afghans, Somalis, and a handful of other nationalities. Refugees identified by UNHCR for third-country resettlement include Iraqis in Jordan, Syria, Turkey, Lebanon, Egypt, Yemen, and the Gulf States; Bhutanese in Nepal; Afghans in Pakistan, Iran, Turkey, Syria, and India; and Iranians in Turkey. In 2013, UNHCR also referred a small number of particularly vulnerable Syrian refugee cases residing in neighboring countries.

As of early 2013, 126,362 Iraqi refugees were registered with UNHCR. There is no internationally agreed-upon definitive number of Iraqi refugees and internally displaced persons due to the fact that not all are registered with UNHCR and they are dispersed throughout the region. UNHCR reports that approximately 1.2 million Iraqis displaced by sectarian violence following the Samarra Mosque bombing of February 2006 remain internally displaced. There are nearly 147,500 Syrian refugees in Iraq, as well as approximately 36,000 refugees and 6,500 asylum seekers of other origins (including Palestinians and Iranian Kurds).

Intense fighting in Syria has caused massive displacement, both internally and to neighboring countries. As of May 15, 2013, there were over 1.5 million Syrian refugees in Lebanon, Jordan, Turkey, Iraq, and Egypt. The United States government is providing assistance to displaced Syrians throughout the region through support to international organizations, such as UNHCR, UNICEF, IOM, ICRC, and WFP, as well as through non-governmental organizations, which are providing critical assistance such as water and sanitation, shelter, and medical care. As of June 17, the United States government had provided more than $800 million in critical humanitarian assistance.

Despite the voluntary repatriation of over 5.7 million Afghan refugees since 2002, Pakistan and Iran continue to host, respectively, approximately 1.6 million and 800,000 registered Afghans, many of whom have resided in these countries for decades. The maintenance of asylum and protection space for those refugees who cannot yet return to Afghanistan while continuing to support voluntary repatriation, is a top priority for the U.S. Government and for UNHCR. In addition to Afghan refugees, some 2-3 million Afghans are believed to live and work in Pakistan and Iran as economic migrants without documentation. Over 10,000 Afghan refugees and asylum seekers are also registered with UNHCR in India. Identifying durable solutions remains an important component of UNHCR's strategy in India. Local integration remains a difficult option due to opposition from host countries such as Bangladesh, Malaysia, Pakistan, and India.

Thousands of ethnic Nepalis in Bhutan were forced out of Bhutan in the early 1990s as a result of the Bhutanese government's policy of "one nation and one people" (also referred to as "Bhutanization"). Despite 17 rounds of formal negotiations between Bhutan and Nepal, and pressure from the United States and other governments to resolve the issue and secure the right of return for genuine Bhutanese nationals, particularly humanitarian cases, to date none have been permitted to return. Due to concerted resettlement efforts commenced in late 2007 by the United States and other resettlement countries, approximately 80,000 of the original population of 108,000 Bhutanese refugees in Nepal have departed after spending two decades in camps in eastern Nepal.

Religious Freedom

Persecution of religious groups is common in many countries in the Middle East and South Asia that are countries of origin for refugee populations entering the United States. State and local government responses to violence against members of religious groups, particularly Muslims and Christians, are often inadequate. Although many of these countries do not have Jewish populations, anti-Semitism is prevalent, and often espoused by governments or religious leaders, especially in Iran.

In Afghanistan, religious freedom is limited due to constitutional contradictions, legislative ambiguity, and interpretations of Islamic law that punish apostasy and blasphemy.

In Pakistan, the penal code includes blasphemy laws that carry punishments ranging from imprisonment to the death penalty. Frequent abuses of these laws negatively affect religious minorities, both Muslims and non-Muslims. In early 2011, two Pakistani senior government officials were killed after speaking out against the application of the blasphemy laws against minorities and others remain under threat from violent extremists.

In Sri Lanka, religious tensions continue to be a problem, and Muslim, Hindu, and Buddhist communities often distrust one another. Incidents such as sporadic attacks against the Christian community and the destruction of a Muslim shrine by Buddhist monks in late 2011 exacerbate such tensions.

In Bhutan, Buddhism is the state's "spiritual heritage," although in the southern areas many citizens openly practice Hinduism. While subtle pressure on non-Buddhists to observe the traditional Buddhist values and some limitations on constructing non-Buddhist religious buildings remain, the government has taken steps to improve religious freedom in the country. Some societal pressures toward non-Buddhists are reflected in official and unofficial efforts to uphold the "spiritual heritage" (Buddhism) of the country.

In Iran, religious groups, including Sunni Muslims, Bahai's, Sufis, Jews, Zoroastrians, and Christians, continue to face official discrimination, harassment, and arrest. Members of the Shia community who express religious views different from those of the government are also subject to harassment and intimidation. The government continues to increase convictions and executions of dissidents, political reformists, and peaceful protesters on the charge of moharebeh (enmity against God) and anti-Islamic propaganda.

Increasing sectarian violence impacts all of Iraq's religious communities, especially the Shia Muslim population. Iraq's minority communities, including Christians, Yezidis, Sabean-Mandaeans, and others, have experienced wide-scale displacement. Some 20 percent of registered Iraqi refugees are members of religious minorities, a figure appreciably larger than their percentage of the overall Iraqi population. As a result, some of these religious communities, along with their ancient languages and customs, are on the verge of disappearing.

In Syria, the government increased its targeting and surveillance of members of faith groups it deemed a "threat," including members of the country's Sunni majority and outlawed Jehovah's Witnesses. This occurred concurrently with the escalation of violent extremist activity as the current civil conflict continues. There were credible reports that the regime targeted citizens based on religious affiliation in mixed neighborhoods in Homs and rural Aleppo. Extrajudicial punishments were common.

In Egypt, the government generally failed to prevent, investigate, or prosecute crimes against members of religious minority groups, especially Coptic Christians – including the recent attack at the Cathedral of St. Mark, the seat of the Coptic Orthodox Pope. This fostered a culture of impunity. Christians, Shiites, Baha'is, and other minorities faced personal and collective discrimination, especially in government employment and the ability to build, renovate, and repair places of worship. The government routinely failed to condemn and sometimes contributed to incendiary speech, including anti-Semitic, anti-Christian, and anti-Shia speech.

In some countries in the region, most notably Afghanistan, Iran, Saudi Arabia, Pakistan, and Egypt, blasphemy, apostasy, and defamation of religion laws are used to restrict religious liberty, constrain the rights of religious minorities, and limit freedom of expression and those accused face threats of violence. Under these governments' interpretations of Islamic law, individuals have their civil rights infringed upon if any member of society files a complaint against them. In most countries in the region Sharia courts decide personal status cases. In Iran, judges in these courts often rule against converts and members of minority religious groups by annulling marriages, transferring child custody, conveying property rights to Muslim family members, infringing upon the civil rights of these individuals, and declaring them wards of the state without any religious identity. Iran and Saudi Arabia are designated by the Department of State as CPCs under the International Religious Freedom Act of 1998 for systematic, ongoing, and egregious violations of religious freedom.

The USRAP provides resettlement access in various ways to refugees who suffer religious persecution. Under the Specter Amendment, Iranian religious minorities designated as Priority 2 category members are considered under a reduced evidentiary standard for establishing a well-founded fear of persecution. Iranian refugees have also gained access to the program through Priority 3. In addition, the USRAP accepts UNHCR and embassy referrals of religious minorities of various nationalities in the region. Nationals of any country, including CPCs, may be referred to the U.S. program by UNHCR or a U.S. embassy for reasons of religious persecution.

Voluntary Repatriation

After the fall of the Taliban, voluntary repatriation to Afghanistan proceeded on a massive scale for several years, both with and without UNHCR assistance. Since 2002, over 5.7 million Afghan refugees have returned, mostly from Pakistan and Iran. Over 4.6 million were assisted by UNHCR in the largest repatriation operation in UNHCR's history. However, the era of mass returns has largely ended, with about 94,000 returning in 2012. The substantial repatriation represents roughly a 20 percent increase in Afghanistan's total population and has taxed the country's capacity to absorb additional refugee returns.

It is unlikely that all of the remaining 2.6 million registered Afghans in Pakistan and Iran will repatriate. UNHCR and IOM's assessment is that the continuing migration of Afghans in both directions across the Afghanistan-Pakistan border is part of a larger process of economic and social migration that has been occurring for centuries. UNHCR is working with the Governments of Pakistan, Afghanistan, and Iran and the international community to develop policies and programs to sustain voluntary returns, while also better managing the residual Afghan population in Pakistan by working towards longer-term protection and migration solutions. IOM is seeking a greater role in border management and in developing regional mechanisms for economic migration that would bolster protection for Afghans. The Government of the Islamic Republic of Afghanistan is working to increase its capacity to help returnees fold back into Afghan economic and social structures and the same time ensuring continued protection for its citizens still seeking refuge abroad. UNHCR, together with the Governments of Afghanistan, Pakistan and Iran agreed to a *Solutions Strategy for Afghan Refugees to Support Voluntary Repatriation, Sustainable Reintegration and Assistance to Host Countries (SSAR)* which provides for the orderly, voluntary return of Afghan refugees and emphasizes the need to fully reintegrate returned refugees into their communities.

Stabilizing the displaced Afghan population – e.g., reintegrating returning refugees and IDPs into the Afghan society, preserving asylum space for refugees in neighboring countries – is critical to regional stability, as well as addressing irregular migration. Through a unique quadripartite consultative process, the Islamic Republics of Afghanistan, Iran, and Pakistan and UNHCR have agreed on a multi-year regional strategy, endorsed by the international community in May 2012 to address assistance to Afghan refugees and returnees, emphasizing cross-border linkages. The Afghan government is also working on a national IDP policy which will seek to address protection, assistance, and durable solutions issues for displaced populations within its borders.

Since 2008, over one million IDPs and refugees have returned to their homes in Iraq, with IDPs composing 78% of these returns. About 86 percent of all returns have been to Baghdad and Diyala, a province northeast of Baghdad. This trend generally matches displacement patterns as over 80 percent of all IDPs and 70 percent of all refugees were displaced from those locations. UNHCR is working with some Iraqis in neighboring countries on an individual basis to facilitate voluntary returns to Iraq. In 2012, nearly 85,000 Iraqi refugees, approximately 56,500 of whom were living in Syria, returned to Iraq and registered for assistance through the Iraqi government or UNHCR.

The United States continues to work with other interested governments in urging the Government of Bhutan to allow for the voluntary repatriation of Bhutanese refugees to Bhutan under acceptable terms and conditions. With the end of the conflict in Sri Lanka, approximately 6,000 refugees have returned. However, the number of Tamils seeking to return from India has decreased. So far in 2013, UNHCR assisted in the voluntary return of 245 Tamil refugees to Sri Lanka.

Local Integration

The SSAR also promotes enhancing support for refugee-hosting communities and providing some alternative stay arrangements for refugees in Afghanistan and Iran. While some progress is being made, few countries in the region offer local integration to refugees. In March 2010, the Government of Pakistan approved the Afghan Management Strategy for the years 2010-2012, which officially permitted Afghan Proof of Registration (POR) cardholders to remain in Pakistan through December 2012. This was subsequently extended to June 30, 2013, deferring the decision until after the May 2013 parliamentary elections. As of late May 2013, Pakistan is formulating its policy for Afghan refugees beyond 2013. As part of the Pakistan implementation of the SSAR and in partnership with the Government of Pakistan and UN agencies, UNHCR launched the Refugee-Affected and Hosting Areas (RAHA) initiative in 2009. This program is widely regarded as a success in addressing Afghan refugee and Pakistani host community needs by rehabilitating areas that have been adversely affected by the presence of Afghan refugee communities over the past 30 years. The United States will continue to work with UNHCR and the Government of Pakistan, including under the SSAR and RAHA, to preserve asylum space and promote alternative stay arrangements. However, at present, local integration is not an available option for most of the remaining Afghan refugees.

Syria hosted over 63,500 UNHCR-registered Iraqi refugees as of February 28, 2013. Iraqis do not need a visa to enter Syria. They receive a stamp upon entry, which allows for six months of residence and should be renewed at the local government offices. Because of the continuing violence in Syria, many Iraqis have fled the country. The Government of Jordan (GOJ) requires visas for Iraqis and has instituted an additional visa category for Iraqis coming to Jordan since unrest broke out in Syria in 2011. Few Iraqis are receiving these visas, but UNHCR and other partners nevertheless report that there are hundreds of new Iraqi arrivals from Syria and Iraq each month. The GOJ continues to preserve first asylum and protection space for Iraqi refugees and remains a generous host.

Iraqis in Syria and Jordan are not legally defined as refugees, but rather as guests. Both governments allow UNHCR to register Iraqis. With help from the international community, the Governments of Syria and Jordan have allowed Iraqi students to enroll in public schools. However, enrollments in both countries have been lower than anticipated. In both Syria and Jordan, Iraqi refugees have access to the public health care systems. Although the Government of Jordan has granted access to several legal labor sectors to Iraqis, few have obtained work permits as they are also required to obtain residency permits, which the GOJ is not issuing to Iraqis. Iraqis do not have access to the legal labor market in Syria.

The Government of Iraq has acknowledged that many Iraqi IDPs will not be able to return to their home communities, and instead require support integrating into their areas of displacement. UNHCR and other international partners are also seeking to support local integration as a viable option for IDPs, but they point out that, in addition to the integration grant, it will be important for displaced Iraqis to be able to access services in their areas of displacement.

While Turkey ratified the 1951 UN Refugee Convention and acceded to its 1967 Protocol, the Turkish government acceded to the Protocol with a geographic limitation acknowledging refugees only from Europe. While most asylum seekers are thus not considered refugees under Turkish law, the Turkish government grants temporary refuge and temporary local integration possibilities to refugees recognized by UNHCR usually pending their referral to a potential resettlement country. As of March 22, 2013, there were 34,471 persons registered with UNHCR Turkey, the majority from Iraq (40%), Afghanistan (26%) and Iran (20%). In addition to the Syrian influx into Turkey over the past year, Turkey has also seen substantial, increased arrivals of Iraqis and Iranians. UNHCRrecognized refugees and asylum seekers in Turkey are assigned to one of 61 satellite cities. Provincial governments are responsible for meeting their basic needs, including by providing access to employment, healthcare, and education although support varies from one location to another. On April 4, 2013, the Turkish Parliament passed the "Foreigners and International Protection Law," which will regulate the entry, exit, and the stay of migrants in the country, along with the scope of international protection for those who seek asylum in Turkey.

Despite the increasing number of asylum seekers and refugees, India does not have a clear national policy for the treatment of refugees, and UNHCR has a limited mandate in the country. In New Delhi, urban refugees face difficult conditions, including discrimination and harassment by the local population, limiting their local integration prospects. India permits UNHCR to assist urban refugees in New Delhi, primarily Burmese, Afghans, and Somalis. India recognizes and aids certain groups, including Sri Lankan Tamils and Tibetans in the 112 camps for Sri Lankans and 39 settlements for Tibetans located throughout the country. The Government of India provides support and benefits to registered Tibetan and Sri Lankan refugees. It also grants work authorization to documented Tibetans. However, Sri Lankan refugees in India do not receive work authorization from the central government but are unofficially allowed to work on the informal economy.

UNHCR has negotiated an agreement with the Government of India whereby India would facilitate access to citizenship for Hindu and Sikh Afghan refugees who meet the standard criteria to acquire Indian citizenship, while UNHCR would pursue resettlement opportunities for other long-staying ethnic Afghan refugees. Naturalization clinics were established to support the citizenship process for Hindu and Sikh Afghans, and UNHCR intensified its efforts to ensure that all eligible refugees had submitted applications for Indian citizenship by December 31, 2009. As a result, over 4,400 applications have been submitted and over 670 Afghans have naturalized.

Third-Country Resettlement

The USRAP anticipates the continued large-scale processing of Iraqis, Bhutanese, and, to a lesser extent, Iranians, during FY 2014.

The United States recognizes that the possibility of third-country resettlement must be available to the most vulnerable Iraqi refugees, and has processing facilities in Amman, Baghdad, Beirut, Cairo, Damascus, and Istanbul. While most Iraqis gain access to the USRAP via a referral from UNHCR, we are also facilitating direct access to the USRAP for Iraqis with close U.S. affiliations in those processing locations where hosting governments permit. The passage of the Refugee Crisis in Iraq Act, enacted January 28, 2008, created new categories of Iraqis who are eligible for direct access (P-2) to the USRAP, both inside and outside Iraq. Currently, beneficiaries of P-2 categories who may seek access to the USRAP in Jordan, Egypt, and Iraq include:

1) Iraqis who work/worked on a full-time basis as interpreters/translators for the U.S. Government, MNF-I in Iraq, or U.S. Forces-Iraq;
2) Iraqis who are/were employed by the U.S. Government in Iraq;
3) Iraqis who are/were employees of an organization or entity closely associated with the U.S. mission in Iraq that has received U.S. Government funding through an official and documented contract, award, grant or cooperative agreement;

4) Iraqis who are/were employed in Iraq by a U.S.-based media organization or non-governmental organization;

5) Spouses, sons, daughters, parents, and siblings of individuals described in the four categories above, or of an individual eligible for a Special Immigrant Visa as a result of his/her employment by or on behalf of the U.S. Government in Iraq, including if the individual is no longer alive, provided that the relationship is verified; and

6) Iraqis who are the spouses, sons, daughters, parents, brothers, or sisters of a citizen of the United States, or who are the spouses or unmarried sons or daughters of a Permanent Resident Alien of the United States, as established by their being or becoming beneficiaries of approved family-based I-130 Immigrant Visa Petitions.

The United States has increased its in-country processing capacity nearly 300 percent since establishing a Resettlement Support Center in Baghdad in FY 2008 and looks to continue to expand that capacity in FY 2013 and FY 2014. Although security and logistical challenges associated with operating an RSC in Iraq limit in-country processing capacity, refugee admissions from Iraq are exceeding those from neighboring countries. Refugee processing in Iraq is a high priority for the United States as it directly benefits Iraqis associated with U.S. efforts in Iraq. DHS continues to devote substantial resources to Iraqi refugee processing and maintains a robust interview schedule in the region.

Middle Eastern and South Asian refugees in most of Europe avail themselves of the asylum systems of the countries in which they are located. In Vienna, however, certain Iranian religious minorities (Baha'is, Zoroastrians, Jews, Mandaeans, and Christians) may be processed for U.S. resettlement using special procedures authorized by the Government of Austria. RSC Vienna has experienced a marked increase in new applications in FY 2011 and FY2012. The Lautenberg legislation expired in September 2012 and was subsequently reauthorized in March 2013, allowing new applications to be filed and adjudicated under Lautenberg guidelines. The United States also processes Iranian religious minorities (primarily Baha'i) and other Iranians in Turkey through special procedures involving fast-track refugee status determination and referral by UNHCR.

Resettlement processing for Bhutanese refugees in Nepal is continuing smoothly and the United States remains committed to considering for resettlement as many refugees as express interest. As of May 2013, UNHCR had referred over 100,000 Bhutanese refugees for resettlement to eight countries and more than 80,000 of these Bhutanese refugees have been resettled to these countries – most notably the United States – since late 2007.

The United States has agreed to join an Australia-led effort to increase resettlement of Afghans from Pakistan, and we anticipate increased UNHCR referrals in coming years. UNHCR currently refers some 300 individuals per year from India, with priority given to those they deem most vulnerable. The majority of referrals are Burmese. UNHCR also refers a very limited number of refugees out of Sri Lanka, mostly Pakistanis. We continue to explore modalities for processing vulnerable Tibetan refugees in the region.

FY 2013 U.S. Admissions

We estimate the admission of approximately 32,000 refugees from the region in FY 2013. These will include some 9,500 Bhutanese, 19,000 Iraqis, 2,000 Iranians and several hundred Afghans, including a small group of women who had been living in Iran processed through the UNHCR Emergency Transit Center in Slovakia.

FY 2014 U.S. Resettlement Program

The proposed regional ceiling for refugees from the Near East and South Asia for FY 2014 is 35,000, including vulnerable Iraqis, Bhutanese, Iranians, Syrians, Pakistanis, and Afghans. We expect individual UNHCR referrals of various religious and ethnic groups in the region, including Assyrians, Mandeans, and Iranian Kurds. In addition, Ahmadi Muslims in many locations and Afghans in the former Soviet Union, Pakistan, India, and elsewhere will be included. Small numbers of Iraqi and other refugee groups who fled Libya are also scheduled for processing. We also expect UNHCR referrals of particularly vulnerable Syrian refugees residing in neighboring countries, given UNHCR's mid-2013 decision that third-country resettlement will play a role in its response to the Syrian refugee crisis.

Proposed FY 2014 Near East/ South Asia Program to Include Arrivals from the Following Categories

Priority 1 Individual Referrals	16,950
Priority 2 Groups	17,000
Priority 3 Family Reunification	50
Total Proposed Ceiling	34,000

IV. DOMESTIC IMPACT OF REFUGEE ADMISSIONS

In FY 2012, the USRAP admitted 58,238 refugees from 56 countries. More than half were originally from either Bhutan or Burma. (See Table 3)

The demographic characteristics of refugee arrivals from the 20 largest source countries (representing 100 percent of total arrivals) in FY 2012 illustrate the variation among refugee groups. The median age of all FY 2012 arrivals was 25 years and ranged from 19 years for arrivals from the Democratic Republic of Congo and Central African Republic to 34 years of age for arrivals from Cuba. In FY 2012, 46.1 percent of all arriving refugees were female and 53.9 percent of all arriving refugees were male. Males predominated among refugees from Eritrea (78.9 percent), Sudan (64.3 percent), and Ethiopia (57.9 percent). (See Table 4)

Of the total arrivals in FY 2012, some 8.9 percent were under the age of five, 23.5 percent were of school age, 68.1 percent were of working age, and 3.1 percent were of retirement age. (See Table 5) Considerable variation among refugee groups can be seen among specific age categories. Refugees under the age of five ranged from a high of 16.2 percent among Central African Republic arrivals to a low of 3.4 percent of those from Iran. The number of school-aged children (from five to 17 years of age) varied from a high of over 45.6 percent of arrivals from the Central African Republic to a low of 10.2 percent of those from Eritrea. The number of working-aged refugees (16 to 64 years of age) varied from a high of 86.5 percent of those from Eritrea to a low of 43.4 percent of individuals from the Central African Republic. Retirement-aged refugees (65 years or older) ranged from a high of 6.5 percent of arrivals from Cuba to a low of less than one percent of those from Burundi and Congo.

During FY 2012, 63 percent of all arriving refugees resettled in 12 states. The majority were placed in Texas (10.2 percent), followed by California (8.9 percent), Michigan (6.2 percent), New York (6.1 percent), Pennsylvania (4.8 percent), and Georgia (4.3 percent). The states of Florida (3.8 percent), Ohio (3.8 percent), Arizona (3.8 percent), Washington (3.7 percent), North Carolina (3.6 percent), and Illinois (3.6 percent) also were in the top twelve states where refugees were resettled. (See Table 6)

Table 3. Refugee Arrivals by Country of Origin Fiscal Year 2012

Country of Origin	Arrival Number	% of Total
Afghanistan	481	0.83%
Bhutan	15,070	25.88%
Burma	14,160	24.31%
Burundi	186	0.32%
Cambodia	6	0.01%
Cameroon	7	0.01%
Central African Republic	136	0.23%
Chad	12	0.02%
China	45	0.08%
Colombia	126	0.22%
Congo	102	0.18%
Cuba	1,948	3.34%
Dem. Rep. Congo	1,863	3.20%
Egypt	13	0.02%
Eritrea	1,346	2.31%
Ethiopia	620	1.06%
Former Soviet Union*	1,129	1.94%
Gabon	1	0.00%
Gambia	2	0.00%
Gaza Strip	7	0.01%
India	2	0.00%
Iran	1,758	3.02%
Iraq	12,163	20.88%
Ivory Coast	33	0.06%
Jordan	3	0.01%
Kenya	23	0.04%
Korea, North	22	0.04%
Kuwait	3	0.01%
Laos	21	0.04%
Liberia	69	0.12%
Libya	5	0.01%
Morocco	2	0.00%
Nepal	47	0.08%
Niger	4	0.01%
Nigeria	2	0.00%
Pakistan	274	0.47%

Country of Origin	Arrival Number	% of Total
Palestine	141	0.24%
Republic of South Sudan	1	0.00%
Rwanda	157	0.27%
Saudi Arabia	1	0.00%
Senegal	5	0.01%
Sierra Leone	1	0.00%
Somalia	4,911	8.43%
South Africa	1	0.00%
Sri Lanka (Ceylon)	55	0.09%
Sudan	1,077	1.85%
Syria	31	0.05%
Tanzania	2	0.00%
Thailand	3	0.01%
Tibet	9	0.02%
Togo	26	0.04%
Tunisia	1	0.00%
Uganda	18	0.03%
Venezuala	4	0.01%
Vietnam	100	0.17%
Zimbabwe	3	0.01%
TOTAL	**58,238**	**100.00%**

Source: Department of State, Bureau of Population, Refugees, and Migration, Refugee
Processing Center.

Table 4. Median Age and Gender of Refugee Arrivals, Fiscal Year 2012

Rank (# of Arrivals)	Country of Origin	Refugees Admitted	Median Age	% Females	% Males
1	Bhutan	15,070	28	49.47%	50.53%
2	Burma	14,160	23	42.82%	57.18%
3	Iraq	12,163	28	47.34%	52.66%
4	Somalia	4,911	22	45.14%	54.86%
5	Cuba	1,948	34	49.54%	50.46%
6	Dem. Rep. Congo	1,863	19	52.23%	47.77%
7	Iran	1,758	32	47.38%	52.62%
8	Eritrea	1,346	26	21.10%	78.90%
9	Former Soviet Union*	1,129	27	51.55%	48.45%

Table 4. (Continued)

Rank (# of Arrivals)	Country of Origin	Refugees Admitted	Median Age	% Females	% Males
10	Sudan	1,077	24	35.65%	64.35%
11	Ethiopia	620	26	42.10%	57.90%
12	Afghanistan	481	23	49.48%	50.52%
13	Pakistan	274	25	43.07%	56.93%
14	Burundi	186	20	51.08%	48.92%
15	Rwanda	157	23	47.13%	52.87%
16	Palestine	141	25	46.10%	53.90%
17	Central African Republic	136	19	51.47%	48.53%
18	Colombia	126	24	55.56%	44.44%
19	Congo	102	23	43.14%	56.86%
20	Vietnam	100	25	49.00%	51.00%
21	All Other Countries	490	27	47.14%	52.86%
TOTAL		58,238	25	46.07%	53.93%

Source: Department of State, Bureau of Population, Refugees, and Migration, Refugee Processing Center.

Table 5. Select Age Categories of Refugee Arrivals, Fiscal Year 2012

Rank (# of Arrivals)	Country of Origin	Under 5 Yrs	School Age (5-17)	Working Age (16-64)	Retirement Age (=or > 65)
1	Bhutan	7.17%	22.91%	70.19%	4.74%
2	Burma	12.36%	20.79%	68.71%	0.97%
3	Iraq	8.62%	22.87%	66.55%	4.71%
4	Somalia	9.81%	31.26%	61.90%	0.94%
5	Cuba	4.11%	20.89%	72.43%	6.52%
6	Dem. Rep. Congo	10.90%	41.12%	53.89%	0.48%
7	Iran	3.36%	13.03%	79.75%	5.69%
8	Eritrea	4.16%	10.25%	86.55%	0.22%
9	Former Soviet Union*	10.01%	27.99%	60.94%	5.58%
10	Sudan	9.47%	25.07%	68.80%	0.28%
11	Ethiopia	7.74%	20.81%	74.03%	0.81%
12	Afghanistan	5.41%	36.80%	63.20%	1.46%
13	Pakistan	9.12%	23.72%	66.79%	1.46%

Rank (# of Arrivals)	Country of Origin	Under 5 Yrs	School Age (5-17)	Working Age (16-64)	Retirement Age (=or > 65)
14	Burundi	12.37%	42.47%	52.15%	0.00%
15	Rwanda	5.73%	40.76%	58.60%	0.64%
16	Palestine	13.48%	24.82%	61.70%	3.55%
17	Central African Republic	16.18%	45.59%	43.38%	1.47%
18	Colombia	9.52%	35.71%	57.94%	3.17%
19	Congo	5.88%	35.29%	65.69%	0.00%
20	Vietnam	6.00%	36.00%	62.00%	2.00%
21	All Other Countries	7.35%	25.71%	69.80%	2.24%
TOTAL		8.94%	23.51%	68.13%	3.12%

Note: Totals may exceed 100 percent due to overlapping age categories.

Source: Department of State, Bureau of Population, Refugees, and Migration, Refugee Processing Center.

Table 6. Refugee Arrivals by State of Initial Resettlement, Fiscal Year 2012

STATE	Refugee Arrivals	Amerasian Arrivals	Total Arrivals	% of Total Arrivals to U.S.
Alabama	145	0	145	0.25%
Alaska	88	0	88	0.15%
Arizona	2,234	0	2,234	3.84%
Arkansas	10	0	10	0.02%
California	5,167	6	5,173	8.88%
Colorado	1,458	0	1,458	2.50%
Connecticut	434	0	434	0.75%
District of Columbia	14	0	14	0.02%
Florida	2,244	0	2,244	3.85%
Georgia	2,516	4	2,520	4.33%
Hawaii	1	0	1	0.00%
Idaho	817	0	817	1.40%
Illinois	2,082	0	2,082	3.57%
Indiana	1,197	0	1,197	2.06%
Iowa	426	5	431	0.74%
Kansas	384	0	384	0.66%

Table 6. (Continued)

STATE	Refugee Arrivals	Amerasian Arrivals	Total Arrivals	% of Total Arrivals to U.S.
Kentucky	1,452	0	1,452	2.49%
Louisiana	187	0	187	0.32%
Maine	203	0	203	0.35%
Maryland	1,239	0	1,239	2.13%
Massachusetts	1,537	4	1,541	2.65%
Michigan	3,594	0	3,594	6.17%
Minnesota	1,738	0	1,738	2.98%
Mississippi	8	0	8	0.01%
Missouri	1,065	0	1,065	1.83%
Montana	1	0	1	0.00%
Nebraska	764	0	764	1.31%
Nevada	470	0	470	0.81%
New Hampshire	363	0	363	0.62%
New Jersey	279	0	279	0.48%
New Mexico	189	0	189	0.32%
New York	3,525	3	3,528	6.06%
North Carolina	2,099	11	2,110	3.62%
North Dakota	555	0	555	0.95%
Ohio	2,245	0	2,245	3.85%
Oklahoma	299	0	299	0.51%
Oregon	691	4	695	1.19%
Pennsylvania	2,809	0	2,809	4.82%
Rhode Island	130	0	130	0.22%
South Carolina	135	0	135	0.23%
South Dakota	646	0	646	1.11%
Tennessee	1,236	0	1,236	2.12%
Texas	5,905	18	5,923	10.17%
Utah	942	0	942	1.62%
Vermont	350	0	350	0.60%
Virginia	1,341	0	1,341	2.30%
Washington	2,165	0	2,165	3.72%

STATE	Refugee Arrivals	Amerasian Arrivals	Total Arrivals	% of Total Arrivals to U.S.
West Virginia	19	0	19	0.03%
Wisconsin	781	4	785	1.35%
Total	58,179	59	58,238	100.00%

Note: Arrival figures do not reflect secondary migration.

Source: Department of State, Bureau of Population, Refugees, and Migration, Refugee Processing Center.

Table 7. Estimated Available Funding for Refugee Processing, Movement, and Resettlement FY 2013 and FY 2014 ($ Millions)

AGENCY	ESTIMATED FY 2013 (BY DEPARTMENT)	ESTIMATED FY 2014 (BY DEPARTMENT)
DEPARTMENT OF HOMELAND SECURITY *United States Citizenship and Immigration Services*		
Refugee Processing 1	$26.3	$32.3
DEPARTMENT OF STATE *Bureau of Population, Refugees, and Migration*		
Refugee Admissions 2, 3	$468.0	$415.0
DEPARTMENT OF HEALTH AND HUMAN SERVICES *Administration for Children and Families, Office of Refugee Resettlement*		
Refugee Resettlement 4	$623.3	$618.8
TOTAL	$1,117.6	$1,066.1

The estimated FY 2014 figures above reflect the President's FY 2014 Budget request and do not include carryover funds from FY 2013.

[1] FY 2014: Includes cost factors to reflect Headquarters facilities rent related to the refugee resettlement program, projected staffing enhancements, and following-to-join refugee processing, in addition to certain ICASS costs.

[2] FY 2013: Includes FY 2013 MRA appropriation of $310 million, $93.9 million in PRM carryover from FY 2012, $58.1 million projected IOM loan collections/carryover, and an estimate of $6 million in prior year MRA recoveries. A portion of these funds will be carried forward into FY 2014.

[3] FY 2014: Includes FY 2014 MRA budget request of $362 million, $47 million in projected IOM loan collections/carryover, and an estimate of $6 million in prior year MRA recoveries. Funds carried forward from FY 2013 will also be available in FY 2014.

[4] FY 2013 and FY 2014: HHS's Office of Refugee Resettlement's (ORR) refugee benefits and services are also provided to asylees, Cuban and Haitian entrants, certain Amerasians from Vietnam, victims of a severe form of trafficking who have received certification or eligibility letters from ORR, and certain family members who are accompanying or following to join victims of severe forms of trafficking, and some victims of torture, as well as Iraqi and Afghan Special Immigrants and their spouses and unmarried children under the age of 21. None of these additional groups is included in the refugee admissions ceiling except Amerasians. This category does not include costs associated with the Unaccompanied Alien Children's Program, Temporary Assistance for Needy Families (TANF), Medicaid, Supplemental Security Income programs, or the Victims of Domestic Trafficking. The estimated FY 2014 figures above reflect the President's FY 2014 Budget request and do not include carryover funds from FY 2013, as HHS does not anticipate any carryover funding from FY 2013.

Table 8. UNHCR Resettlement Statistics by Resettlement Country CY 2012 Admissions

RESETTLEMENT COUNTRY	TOTAL	PERCENT OF TOTAL RESETTLED
United States	53,349	76.57%
Australia	4,989	7.16%
Canada	4,803	6.89%
Sweden	1,545	2.22%
Norway	1,104	1.58%
United Kingdom	989	1.42%
New Zealand	775	1.11%
Finland	755	1.08%
Denmark	320	0.46%
Germany	313	0.45%
Netherlands	262	0.38%
France	83	0.12%
Spain	80	0.11
Switzerland	54	0.08%
Slovakia	50	0.07%
Ireland	40	0.06%
Brazil	39	0.06%
Czech Rep.	25	0.04%
Portugal	21	0.03%
Rep. Of Korea	20	0.03%
Argentina	18	0.03%
Italy	9	0.01%
Iceland	9	0.01%

RESETTLEMENT COUNTRY	TOTAL	PERCENT OF TOTAL RESETTLED
Uruguay	9	0.01%
Estonia	4	0.01%
Chile	3	0.00%
Hungary	1	0.00%
TOTAL	69,669	100.00%

End Notes

[1] Detailed discussion of the anticipated social and economic impact, including secondary migration, of the admission of refugees to the United States is being provided in the *Report to the Congress* of the Refugee Resettlement Program, Office of Refugee Resettlement, Department of Health and Human Services.

[2] These proposed figures assume enactment by Congress of the President's Budget levels related to the U.S. Refugee Admissions Program elements.

[3] Referrals of North Koreans and Palestinians require State Department and DHS/USCIS concurrence before they may be granted access to the USRAP.

[4] Formerly known as Overseas Processing Entities (OPEs)

[5] This petition is used to file for the relatives of refugees and asylees, known as Visa 93 and Visa 92 cases respectively. The Refugee Admissions Program handles only Visa 93 cases, which are counted within the annual refugee admissions ceiling. Visa 92 cases are not considered to be refugee admissions cases and are not counted in the number of refugees admitted annually.

[6] Nearly 6,500 of these exemptions pertained to Burmese applicants who had associations with groups that met the statutory definition of an undesignated "terrorist organization" in Section 212(a)(3)(B). Approximately 5,000 of the exemptions related to applicants who provided material support to a terrorist organization under duress – for example, Iraqi applicants who paid a ransom for a kidnapped family member.

In: Refugees Around the World
Editor: Jarod Humphrey

ISBN: 978-1-63117-896-2
© 2014 Nova Science Publishers, Inc.

Chapter 2

REFUGEE ADMISSIONS
AND RESETTLEMENT POLICY*

Andorra Bruno

SUMMARY

A refugee is a person fleeing his or her country because of persecution or a well-founded fear of persecution on account of race, religion, nationality, membership in a particular social group, or political opinion. Typically, the annual number of refugees that can be admitted into the United States, known as the refugee ceiling, and the allocation of these numbers by region are set by the President after consultation with Congress at the start of each fiscal year. For FY2013, the worldwide refugee ceiling is 70,000, with 67,000 admissions numbers allocated among the regions of the world and 3,000 numbers comprising an unallocated reserve. An unallocated reserve is to be used if, and where, a need develops for refugee slots in excess of the allocated numbers. The FY2013 regional allocations are, as follows: Africa (12,000), East Asia (17,000), Europe and Central Asia (2,000), Latin America/Caribbean (5,000), and Near East/South Asia (31,000).

Overseas processing of refugees is conducted through a system of three priorities for admission. Priority 1 comprises cases involving persons facing compelling security concerns. Priority 2 comprises cases

---

* This is an edited, reformatted and augmented version of a Congressional Research Service publication, CRS Report for Congress RL31269, prepared for Members and Committees of Congress, from www.crs.gov, dated August 8, 2013.

involving persons from specific groups of special humanitarian concern to the United States (e.g., Iranian religious minorities). Priority 3 comprises family reunification cases involving close relatives of persons admitted as refugees or granted asylum.

Special legislative provisions facilitate relief for certain refugee groups. The "Lautenberg Amendment," which was first enacted in 1989, allows certain former Soviet and Indochinese nationals to qualify for refugee status based on their membership in a protected category with a credible fear of persecution. In 2004, Congress amended the Lautenberg Amendment to add the "Specter Amendment," which requires the designation of categories of Iranian religious minorities whose cases are to be adjudicated under the Lautenberg Amendment's reduced evidentiary standard. Subsequent laws extended the Lautenberg Amendment, as amended by the Specter Amendment. Most recently, the Consolidated and Further Continuing Appropriations Act, 2013 (P.L. 113-6) extends the Lautenberg Amendment through September 30, 2013.

The Department of Health and Human Services' Office of Refugee Resettlement (HHS/ORR) administers an initial transitional assistance program for temporarily dependent refugees and Cuban/Haitian entrants. The final FY2013 appropriation for refugee and entrant assistance in P.L. 113-6 is $1.016 billion; after adjustments for the rescission and the sequestration, FY2013 funding totals $999.4 million.

BACKGROUND AND DEFINITIONS

The admission of refugees to the United States and their resettlement here are authorized by the Immigration and Nationality Act (INA), as amended by the Refugee Act of 1980.[1] The 1980 Act had two basic purposes: (1) to provide a uniform procedure for refugee admissions; and (2) to authorize federal assistance to resettle refugees and promote their self-sufficiency. The intent of the legislation was to end an ad hoc approach to refugee admissions and resettlement that had characterized U.S. refugee policy since World War II.

Under the INA, a *refugee* is a person who is outside his or her country and who is unable or unwilling to return because of persecution or a well-founded fear of persecution on account of race, religion, nationality, membership in a particular social group, or political opinion.[2] In special circumstances, a refugee also may be a person who is within his or her country and who is persecuted or has a well-founded fear of persecution on account of race, religion, nationality, membership in a particular social group, or political opinion. Excluded from the INA definition of a refugee is any person who participated in the persecution of another.[3]

Refugees are processed and admitted to the United States from abroad. The Department of State (DOS) handles overseas processing of refugees and U.S. Citizenship and Immigration Services (USCIS) of the Department of Homeland Security (DHS) makes final determinations about eligibility for admission. Separate provision is made in the INA for the granting of *asylum* on a case-by-case basis to aliens who are physically present in the United States or at a land border or port of entry and who meet the definition of a refugee.[4] After one year in refugee status in the United States, refugees are required to apply to adjust to lawful permanent resident (LPR) status.[5]

REFUGEE ADMISSIONS

The United States aims to consider for resettlement at least half of the refugees referred by the United Nations High Commissioner for Refugees (UNHCR) for resettlement worldwide each year, depending on the availability of funding. By law, the annual number of refugee admissions and the allocation of these numbers by region of the world are set by the President after consultation with Congress.[6] Each year, the President submits a report to the House of Representatives and the Senate, known as the *consultation document*, which contains the Administration's proposed worldwide refugee ceiling and regional allocations for the upcoming fiscal year.[7] Following congressional consultations on the Administration's proposal, the President issues a Presidential Determination setting the refugee numbers for that year.[8] *Table 1* shows refugee admissions ceilings and regional allocations for FY2002-FY2013.

The U.S. refugee program was greatly impacted by the terrorist attacks of September 11, 2001. In the aftermath of those attacks, a review of refugee-related security procedures was undertaken, refugee admissions were briefly suspended, and enhanced security measures were implemented. As a result of these and other factors, actual refugee admissions plunged, declining from an FY2001 total of 69,886 to an FY2002 total of 27,131 and an FY2003 total of 28,403 (see last row of *Table 1* for actual admissions since FY2002).[9]

Admissions have rebounded since FY2002 and FY2003, totaling over 70,000 in each of FY2009 and FY2010. As shown in *Table 1*, however, there were significantly lower levels of admissions in FY2011 (56,424) and FY2012 (58,238). The FY2013 consultation document attributed the shortfalls in refugee arrivals in FY2011 and FY2012 largely to new security requirements and anticipated a rebound in FY2013:

> In the last several years, USRAP [the U.S. Refugee Admissions Program] has incorporated additional security enhancements to safeguard the resettlement program from fraud and national security risks. These changes led to delays in bringing refugees to the United States and the delays, in turn, resulted in a decreased number of refugee arrivals in FY 2011 and 2012. In FY 2010, the United States admitted over 73,000 refugees. That number dipped to just over 56,000 in FY 2011 and this year's [FY2012] admissions total will be only slightly higher. Strides have been made throughout FY 2012 to improve interagency cooperation and streamline other parts of the process so that bona fide refugees gain entry to the United States. Because improvements to the security checks were not implemented until March 2012, refugee arrivals lagged in the early part of the fiscal year and began to increase in May 2012. Since then, arrivals have steadily risen. Increases are expected to continue in August and September [2012] and arrival numbers in FY 2013 should be closer to the proposed ceiling.[10]

FY2013 Refugee Ceiling and Allocations

On September 28, 2012, President Obama signed the Presidential Determination setting the FY2013 worldwide refugee ceiling and regional levels.[11] As indicated in *Table 1*, the FY2013 ceiling is 70,000. The ceiling and allocations in the FY2013 Presidential Determination are identical to those in the FY2013 consultation document.

The FY2013 refugee ceiling of 70,000 includes 67,000 admissions numbers allocated among the regions of the world and an unallocated reserve of 3,000 numbers. An unallocated reserve is to be used if, and where, a need develops for refugee slots in excess of the allocated numbers. This has occurred in recent years, as detailed in *Table 1*.

Africa has been allocated 12,000 refugee admissions numbers for FY2013. The FY2012 allocation to the region was also 12,000, and FY2012 admissions totaled 10,608.[12]

Table 1. Refugee Admissions Ceilings and Regional Allocations, FY2002-FY2013

Region	FY2002	FY2003	FY2004	FY2005	FY2006	FY2007	FY2008	FY2009	FY2010	FY2011	FY2012	FY2013
Africa	22,000	20,000	30,000[b]	21,000[c]	20,000	22,000	16,000	12,000	15,500	15,000	12,000	12,000
East Asia	4,000	4,000	8,500[b]	13,000	15,000	16,000[d]	20,000	20,500[f]	18,000[g]	19,000	18,000	17,000
Europe and Central Asia[a]	26,000	16,500	13,000	15,500[c]	15,000	6,500	3,000	2,500	2,500	2,000	2,000	2,000
Latin America/Caribbean	3,000	2,500	3,500	7,000[c]	5,000	5,000	5,000[e]	5,500[f]	5,500[g]	5,500	5,500	5,000
Near East/South Asia	15,000	7,000	3,000[b]	3,500[c]	5,000	9,000[d]	28,000	39,500[f]	38,000[g]	35,500	35,500	31,000
Unallocated	—	20,000	12,000[b]	10,000[c]	10,000	11,500[d]	8,000[e]	—[f]	500	3,000	3,000	3,000
Total ceilings	70,000	70,000	70,000	70,000	70,000	70,000	80,000	80,000	80,000	80,000	76,000	70,000
Actual admissions	27,131	28,403	52,873	53,813	41,223	48,282	60,191	74,654	73,311	56,424	58,238	NA

Sources: For ceiling and allocation data: PD 2000-32, September 29, 2000; PD 02-04, November 21, 2001; PD 03-02, October 16, 2002; PD 2004-06, October 21, 2003; PD 2004-53, September 30, 2004; PD 2006-3, October 24, 2005; PD 2007-1, October 11, 2006; PD 2008-1, October 2, 2007; PD 2008-29, September 30, 2008; PD 2009- 32, September 30, 2009; PD 2011-02, October 8, 2010; PD 2011-17, September 30, 2011; PD 2012–17, September 28, 2012. U.S. Department of State, U.S. Department of Justice, and U.S. Department of Health and Human Services, Proposed Refugee Admissions … , Fiscal Years 2002-2013. For actual admissions data: U.S. Department of State, Bureau of Population, Refugees and Migration.

a For FY2002-FY2003, separate sub-allocations were provided for the former Yugoslavia and the Former Soviet Union (FSU); they are combined here.

b Of the FY2004 ceiling of 70,000, 50,000 numbers were originally allocated by region and 20,000 were unallocated. The unallocated reserve was tapped during the year to provide 8,000 additional numbers to Africa, East Asia, and Near East/South Asia.

^c Of the FY2005 ceiling of 70,000, 50,000 numbers were originally allocated by region and 20,000 were unallocated. The unallocated reserve was tapped during the year to provide 10,000 additional numbers to Africa, Europe and Central Asia, Latin America/Caribbean, and Near East/South Asia.

^d Of the FY2007 ceiling of 70,000, 50,000 numbers were originally allocated by region and 20,000 were unallocated. The unallocated reserve was tapped during the year to provide 8,500 additional numbers to East Asia and Near East/South Asia.

^e Of the FY2008 ceiling of 80,000, 70,000 numbers were originally allocated by region and 10,000 were unallocated. The unallocated reserve was tapped during the year to provide 2,000 additional numbers to Latin America/Caribbean.

^f Of the FY2009 ceiling of 80,000, 75,000 numbers were originally allocated by region and 5,000 were unallocated. The unallocated reserve was tapped during the year to provide 5,000 additional numbers to East Asia, Latin America/Caribbean, and Near East/South Asia.

^g Of the FY2010 ceiling of 80,000, 75,000 numbers were originally allocated by region and 5,000 were unallocated. The unallocated reserve was tapped during the year to provide 4,500 additional numbers to East Asia, Latin America/Caribbean, and Near East/South Asia.

For Africa, as for all regions, the FY2013 allocation is intended to cover previously approved refugees in the pipeline as well as new cases. FY2013 admissions are expected to come primarily from East and Southern Africa and to include Somalis and Eritreans, among others.

East Asia's FY2013 allocation is 17,000, compared to an FY2012 allocation of 18,000. FY2012 admissions totaled 14,366. FY2013 admissions are expected to consist primarily of Burmese refugees living in Thailand and Malaysia.

Europe and Central Asia have a combined FY2013 allocation of 2,000 refugee numbers, the same as in FY2012. In FY2012, admissions totaled 1,129. The 2013 allocation includes projected admissions of "Lautenberg Amendment" cases from the former Soviet Union (discussed below).

The FY2013 allocation for Latin America and the Caribbean is 5,000, compared to an FY2012 allocation of 5,500. FY2012 admissions totaled 2,078. Cubans account for the vast majority of admissions from this region.

The Near East/South Asia FY2013 allocation is 31,000, a decrease from the FY2012 allocation of 35,500. FY2012 admissions totaled 30,057. FY2013 admissions are expected to include Iraqis, Bhutanese, Iranians, Pakistanis, and Afghans.

Refugee Processing Priorities

DOS is responsible for overseas processing of refugees. Generally, it arranges for a nongovernmental organization (NGO), an international organization, or U.S. embassy contractors to manage a Resettlement Support Center (RSC) that assists in refugee processing. RSC staff conduct pre-screening interviews of prospective refugees and prepare cases for submission to USCIS, which handles refugee adjudications. Overseas refugee processing is conducted through a system of three priorities for admission. These priorities are separate and distinct from whether such persons qualify for refugee status.

Priority 1 covers refugees for whom resettlement seems to be the appropriate durable solution, who are referred to the U.S. refugee program by UNHCR, a U.S. embassy, or a designated NGO. Such persons often have compelling protection needs, and may be in danger of attack or of being returned to the country they fled. All nationalities are eligible for this priority.

Priority 2 covers groups of special humanitarian concern to the United States. It includes specific groups that may be defined by their nationalities, clans, ethnicities, or other characteristics. Unlike Priority 1 cases, individuals falling under Priority 2 are able to access the U.S. refugee program without a UNHCR, embassy, or NGO referral. Some P-2 groups, such as Cuban dissidents and certain former Soviet nationals ("Lautenberg Amendment" cases, discussed below), are processed in their country of origin. Other Priority 2 groups are processed outside their country of origin. These include Iranian religious minorities ("Specter Amendment" cases, discussed below) processed in Austria and Turkey, and Burmese in refugee camps in Thailand. Another P-2 group, Iraqis associated with the United States, is eligible for in-country processing in Iraq as well as processing outside that country.[13]

Priority 3 covers family reunification cases. Refugee applications under Priority 3 are based upon an *affidavit of relationship* (AOR) filed by an eligible relative in the United States. The Priority 3 program is limited to designated nationalities. For FY2013, Priority 3 processing is available to nationals of 22 countries.[14] Individuals falling under Priority 3, like those falling under Priority 2, are able to access the U.S. refugee program without a UNHCR, embassy, or NGO referral.

The Priority 3 program has changed over the years. Since FY2004, qualifying family members have been the spouses, unmarried children under age 21, and parents of persons who were admitted to the United States as refugees or granted asylum.[15] On October 22, 2008, the U.S. refugee program stopped accepting applications under Priority 3.[16] Earlier in 2008, processing of Priority 3 cases was suspended in certain locations in Africa "due to indications of extremely high rates of fraud obtained through pilot DNA testing."[17] Priority 3 processing resumed at the beginning of FY2013 with a new AOR form and requirement for DNA evidence of certain claimed biological parent-child relationships. According to the FY2013 consultation document, the Priority 3 program will be closely monitored "for any indication of new attempts at such fraud."[18]

Refugee Adjudications

USCIS is responsible for adjudicating refugee cases. It makes determinations about whether an individual qualifies for refugee status and is otherwise admissible to the United States. In the past, the majority of refugee adjudications were conducted by USCIS officers on temporary duty from domestic asylum offices. Today, these adjudications are handled by USCIS officers in the Refugee Corps.

Admissibility of Refugees

In order to be admitted to the United States, a prospective refugee must be *admissible* under immigration law. The INA sets forth various grounds of inadmissibility, which include health-related grounds, security-related grounds, public charge (i.e., indigence), and lack of proper documentation.[19] Some inadmissibility grounds (public charge, lack of proper documentation) are not applicable to refugees. Others can be waived for humanitarian purposes, to assure family unity, or when it is otherwise in the public interest.[20] Of particular relevance to the admission of refugees are certain health-related and security-related grounds of inadmissibility.

Under the INA health-related grounds of inadmissibility, an alien who is determined, in accordance with Department of Health and Human Services (HHS) regulations, to have a communicable disease of public health significance is inadmissible. Until recently, human immunodeficiency virus (HIV) infection was defined to be one of these diseases, although HIV-infected refugees could apply for a waiver. In 2008, Congress amended the INA to eliminate the reference to HIV infection as a health-related ground of inadmissibility.[21] And effective January 4, 2010, the Centers for Disease Control and Prevention (CDC) of HHS amended its regulations to remove HIV infection from the definition of a communicable disease of public health significance.[22]

Since 1990, the security-related grounds of inadmissibility in the INA have expressly included terrorism-related grounds. Over the years, the terrorism-related grounds have been amended to lower the threshold for how substantial, apparent, and immediate an alien's support for a terrorist activity or organization may be for the alien to be rendered inadmissible.[23] Among the current terrorism-related grounds, an alien is generally inadmissible for engaging in terrorist activity if he or she gives any material support, such as a safe house, transportation, communications, or funds, to a terrorist organization or any of its members or to a person engaged in terrorist activity. The Secretary of State or the Secretary of DHS, after consultation with the other and the Attorney General, may exercise discretionary waiver authority over certain terrorism-related grounds of inadmissibility. Both the Secretary of State and the Secretary of DHS have exercised this waiver authority with respect to certain categories of individuals.

The Consolidated Appropriations Act, 2008, enacted in December 2007, specifies groups that, for purposes of the INA terrorism-related grounds of inadmissibility, are not to be considered terrorist organizations on the basis of past acts. [24] Thus, a prospective refugee who was a member of, or provided support to, one of these groups would not be inadmissible on the basis of those actions. More broadly, the Consolidated Appropriations Act expands the discretionary authority of the Secretary of State and the Secretary of DHS to grant waivers of the terrorism-related grounds of inadmissibility generally.

Special Refugee Provisions

Lautenberg Amendment and Specter Amendment

The "Lautenberg Amendment" is a provision of the FY1990 Foreign Operations Appropriations Act. It requires the Attorney General to designate categories of former Soviet and Indochinese nationals for whom less evidence is needed to prove refugee status, and provides for adjustment to permanent resident status of certain Soviet and Indochinese nationals granted parole after being denied refugee status.[25] Applicants for refugee status under the special provision are required to prove that they are members of a protected category with a credible, but not necessarily individual, fear of persecution. By contrast, the INA requires prospective refugees to establish a well-founded fear of persecution on a case-by-case basis.

The Lautenberg Amendment has been regularly extended in appropriations acts, although there have often been gaps between extensions. The Consolidated Appropriations Act, 2004, in addition to extending the amendment through FY2004, amended the Lautenberg Amendment to add a new provision known as the "Specter Amendment."[26] The Specter Amendment requires the designation of categories of Iranian nationals, specifically religious minorities, for whom less evidence is needed to prove refugee status. The Consolidated Appropriations Act, 2010, extended the Lautenberg Amendment, including the Specter Amendment, through FY2010.[27] For FY2011, Congress extended the amendment only until June 1, 2011,[28] and it temporarily lapsed on that date. It was re-enacted for FY2012 and for FY2013, and is now in effect through September 30, 2013.[29]

Vietnamese Refugees

The "McCain Amendment," which is no longer in effect, was first enacted in the FY1997 Omnibus Consolidated Appropriations Act.[30] It covered certain adult children, whose parents were Vietnamese re-education camp survivors and had been accepted for U.S. refugee resettlement. The amendment made the adult children eligible for U.S. refugee resettlement. It was subsequently amended and extended through FY1999.

In November 1999, the McCain Amendment was re-enacted in revised form for FY2000 and FY2001 in the Consolidated Appropriations Act, 2000.[31] As revised, it applied to the adult children of a re-education camp survivor who was residing in the United States or awaiting departure from Vietnam and who, after April 1995, was accepted for U.S. refugee resettlement or for admission as an immediate relative immigrant. The April 1995 date restriction did not apply to children who were previously denied refugee resettlement because their documents did not show continuous co-residency with their parent.

Legislation to amend and extend the provision through FY2003 was approved by the 107th Congress in May 2002.[32] This law eliminated the existing April 1995 date restriction. Thus, children who were previously denied refugee resettlement for reasons other than co-residency could also have their cases reconsidered. This revised provision, which was regularly extended,[33] is sometimes referred to as the "McCain-Davis Amendment." The McCain-Davis Amendment was last extended, through FY2010, by the Omnibus Appropriations Act, 2009.[34] This extension was repealed, however, by the Consolidated Appropriations Act, 2010,[35] and the McCain amendment is no longer in effect.

REFUGEE RESETTLEMENT ASSISTANCE

The Department of Health and Human Services' Office of Refugee Resettlement (HHS/ORR), within the Administration for Children and Families (ACF), administers an initial transitional assistance program for temporarily dependent refugees and Cuban/Haitian entrants. Since its establishment in 1980, the refugee resettlement program has been justified on the grounds that the admission of refugees is a federal decision, entailing some federal responsibility. Unlike immigrants who enter through family or employment ties, refugees are admitted on humanitarian grounds, and there is no requirement that they demonstrate economic self-sufficiency.

For FY2012, appropriations for ORR refugee assistance totaled $768.3 million. For FY2013, the Consolidated and Further Continuing Appropriations Act, 2013, appropriates $1.016 billion for refugee assistance;[36] after adjustments for the rescission and the sequestration, FY2013 funding totals $999.4 million, according to ACF.[37] *Table 2* details refugee resettlement funding for FY2003-FY2013.

Table 2. Refugee Resettlement Funding, FY2003-FY2013
(budget authority in millions)

Programs	FY04 Actual	FY05 Actual	FY06 Actual	FY07 Enacted	FY08 Enacted[a]	FY09 Estimate	FY10 Enacted	FY11 Enacted	FY12 Actual	FY13[b]
Transitional/Cash and Medical Services	$169.0	$205.0	$265.4	$265.5	$301.3	$282.3	$353.3	$352.6	$323.2	$401.1
Victims of Trafficking[c]	9.9	9.9	9.8	9.8	10.0	9.8	9.8	9.8	9.8	9.3
Social Services	152.2	152.2	153.9	154.0	156.7	154.0	154.0	153.7	124.3	149.9
Victims of Torture[d]	9.9	9.9	9.8	9.8	10.0	10.8	11.1	11.1	11.0	10.7
Preventive Health	4.8	4.8	4.7	4.7	4.8	4.7	4.7	4.7	4.7	4.6
Targeted Assistance	49.0	49.1	48.6	48.6	49.5	48.6	48.6	48.5	28.1	47.6
Unaccompanied Alien Children[e]	52.8	53.8	77.2	95.3	135.0	123.1	149.4	149.1	267.2	376.1
Total[f]	$447.6	$484.7	$569.4	$587.8	$667.3	$633.4	$730.9	$729.5	$768.3	$999.4

Sources: U.S. Department of Health and Human Services, Administration for Children and Families, Justifications of Estimates for Appropriations Committees, Fiscal Years 2005-2014; U.S. Department of Health and Human Services, Administration for Children and Families, ACF All-Purpose Table, 2005-2007, 2012-2013; U.S. Congress, Conference Committees, Departments of Transportation and Housing and Urban Development, and Related Agencies Appropriations Act, 2010, conference report to accompany H.R. 3288, 111th Cong., 1st sess., H.Rept. 111-366, Labor-Health and Human Services-Education funding table, p. 1292.

[a] Amounts do not reflect recission.

[b] Amounts reflect recission and sequestration.

[c] Funding used primarily for administrative cost of certifying that an alien is a trafficking victim for purposes of receiving benefits and services.

[d] Funding used for rehabilitation services, social services, and legal services for torture victims and for provision of research and training to health care providers.

[e] The Homeland Security Act of 2002 (P.L. 107-296) transferred functions under U.S. immigration law related to the care of unaccompanied alien children from the then-INS to HHS/ORR

[f] Sum of listed amounts may not equal total due to rounding.

ORR-funded refugee assistance activities include refugee cash and medical assistance, social services to help refugees become socially and economically self-sufficient, and targeted assistance for impacted areas. Special refugee cash assistance (RCA) and refugee medical assistance (RMA) are the heart of the refugee program, accounting for a greater portion of the ORR annual budget than any other activity (see *Table 2*). RCA and RMA, which in most cases are administered by the states, are intended to help needy refugees who are ineligible to receive benefits from mainstream federal assistance programs. RCA and RMA are currently available to refugees for eight months after entry.[38] RMA benefits are based on the state's Medicaid program, and RCA payments are now based on the state's Temporary Assistance for Needy Families (TANF) payment to a family unit of the same size.[39]

The ORR program was significantly affected by the 1996 welfare reform act and subsequent amendments.[40] Prior to this legislation, refugees who otherwise met the requirements of federal public assistance programs were immediately and indefinitely eligible to participate in them just like U.S. citizens.

Now, refugees and other specified humanitarian entrants are subject to time limits. *Table 3* summarizes the time limits on refugee eligibility for four major public assistance programs.

Table 3. Refugee Eligibility for Major Federal Public Assistance Programs

Program	Eligibility
Supplemental Security Income (SSI) for the Aged, Blind and Disabled	Eligible for seven years after entry.[a]
Medicaid (non-emergency care)	Eligible for seven years after entry, then state option.
TANF	Eligible for five years after entry, then state option.
Supplemental Nutrition Assistance Program (SNAP) (formerly, Food Stamps)	Eligible without time limits.

[a] A temporary provision (in P.L. 110-328, September 30, 2008) extended to nine years (during FY2009 through FY2011) the period of eligibility of certain refugees and others for SSI benefits, provided that specified criteria were met.

APPENDIX. REFUGEE ADMISSIONS BY REGION, FY1987-FY2012

FY	Africa	EastAsia	Eastern Europe	Former Soviet Union	Latin America/ Caribbean	Near East/ South Asia	Total
1987	1,990	40,099	8,396	3,699	323	10,021	64,528
1988	1,593	35,371	7,510	20,411	3,230[a]	8,368	76,483
1989	1,902	45,722	8,752	39,602	4,116[a]	6,976[a]	107,070
1990	3,453	51,604[a]	6,094	50,628	5,308[a]	4,979	122,066
1991	4,420	53,522	6,837	39,226	4,042[a]	5,342	113,389
1992	5,470	51,899	2,915	61,397	3,947[a]	6,903	132,531
1993	6,967	49,817	2,582	48,773	4,322[a]	6,987	119,448
1994	5,860	43,564	7,707	43,854	6,156	5,840	112,981
1995	4,827	36,987	10,070	35,951	7,629	4,510	99,974
1996	7,604	19,321	12,145	29,816	3,550	3,967	76,403
1997	6,065	8,594	21,401	27,331	2,996	4,101	70,488
1998	6,887	10,854	30,842	23,557	1,627	3,313	77,080
1999	13,043	10,206	38,658	17,410	2,110	4,098	85,525
2000	17,561	4,561	22,561	15,103	3,232	10,129	73,147
2001	19,020	34,163	15,794	15,978	2,975	11,956	69,886
2002	2,551	3,512	5,459	9,969	1,934	3,706	27,131
2003	10,714	1,724	2,506	8,744	455	4,260	28,403
2004	29,104	8,084	9,254[b]		3,577	2,854	52,873
2005	20,745	12,076	11,316[b]		6,699	2,977	53,813
2006	18,126	5,659	10,456[b]		3,264	3,718	41,223
2007	17,483	15,643	4,560[b]		2,976	7,620	48,282
2008	8,935	19,489	2,343[b]		4,277	25,147	60,191
2009	9,670	19,850	1,997[b]		4,857	38,280	74,654
2010	13,305	17,716	1,526[b]		4,982	35,782	73,311
2011	7,685	17,367	1,228[b]		2,976	27,168	56,424
2012	10,608	14,366	1,129 [b]		2,078	30,057	58,238

Source: U.S. Department of State, Bureau of Population, Refugees and Migration.

Notes: Data for 2001-2012 are as of July 31, 2013. Data for earlier years may not reflect all subsequent adjustments.

[a] Includes refugees admitted under the Private Sector Initiative (PSI), most of whom were Cuban.

[b] Beginning in FY2004, the categories of Eastern Europe and the Former Soviet Union were combined into a single category, Europe and Central Asia. These are the total admissions under that category.

End Notes

[1] The INA is Act of June 27, 1952, ch. 477, codified, as amended, at 8 U.S.C. §§1101 et seq. The Refugee Act is P.L. 96-212, March 17, 1980.

[2] This definition conforms with the definition used in the United Nations Convention and Protocol relating to the status of refugees.

[3] INA §101(a)(42).

[4] For further information on asylum, see CRS Report R41753, Asylum and "Credible Fear" Issues in U.S. Immigration Policy, by Ruth Ellen Wasem.

[5] INA §209(a). Asylees (those granted asylum) may apply for LPR status after one year, but are not required to do so. There are no numerical limitations on refugee or asylee adjustments of status.

[6] INA §207(a).

[7] The consultation document for FY2013 is U.S. Department of State, U.S. Department of Homeland Security, and U.S. Department of Health and Human Services, Proposed Refugee Admissions for Fiscal Year 2013: Report to the Congress, http://www.state.gov/documents/organization/198157.pdf (hereinafter cited as Proposed Refugee Admissions for Fiscal Year 2013).

[8] Asylees are not included in the refugee ceiling. There are no numerical limitations on the granting of asylum.

[9] Refugee admissions had not been at or below the FY2002 or FY2003 levels since FY1977, when admissions totaled about 20,000. From FY1979 through FY2001, annual refugee admissions totaled more than 60,000. For annual data on refugee admissions by region since FY1987, see the Appendix at the end of this report.

[10] Proposed Refugee Admissions for Fiscal Year 2013, pp. iv-v.

[11] U.S. President [Obama], "Fiscal Year 2013 Refugee Admissions Numbers and Authorizations of In-Country Refugee Status ...," Presidential Determination No. 2012–17 of September 28, 2012, 77 Federal Register, pp. 61507-61508, October 10, 2012.

[12] See Appendix for annual refugee admissions numbers by region since FY1987.

[13] The Refugee Crisis in Iraq Act of 2007 (Division A, Title XII, Subtitle C of P.L. 110-181, January 28, 2008) designates certain Iraqis for P-2 processing.

[14] The countries are Afghanistan, Bhutan, Burma, Burundi, Central African Republic, Chad, Colombia, Cuba, Democratic People's Republic of Korea (DPRK), Democratic Republic of Congo (DRC), Eritrea, Ethiopia, Haiti, Iran, Iraq, Republic of Congo (ROC), Somalia, South Sudan, Sri Lanka, Sudan, Uzbekistan, and Zimbabwe. Proposed Refugee Admissions for Fiscal Year 2013, p. 13.

[15] During the late 1990s, the State Department found that a large number of Priority 3 applications were received from persons who did not qualify for refugee status and that there was a significant amount of fraud associated with these applications. To address these problems, the U.S. government reduced the number of nationalities eligible for such refugee slots. For FY2003, four nationalities were eligible for Priority 3 processing. For FY2004, the Priority 3 program was revised on a pilot basis. To simultaneously broaden access to the program and continue to address concerns about fraud, the number of eligible nationalities was increased to nine, while the types of qualifying relationships were restricted. As noted above, eligibility for Priority 3 currently requires a qualifying relationship with an individual who was admitted to the United States as a refugee or granted asylum. Prior to FY2004, this processing priority was available to those with qualifying relationships with a much wider range of legal U.S. residents without regard to how these residents gained

admission to the United States. In another change, since FY2004, children have to be under age 21 to be eligible for Priority 3. In the past, this processing priority was also available to older unmarried sons and daughters. These changes to the Priority 3 qualifying relationships have remained in place since FY2004.

[16] U.S. Department of State, Bureau of Population, Refugees, and Migration, "Fraud in the Refugee Family Reunification (Priority Three) Program," fact sheet, December 4, 2008.

[17] Proposed Refugee Admissions for Fiscal Year 2013, p. 12.

[18] Ibid., p. 12.

[19] For further information on the grounds of inadmissibility generally, see CRS Report R41104, Immigration Visa Issuances and Grounds for Exclusion: Policy and Trends, by Ruth Ellen Wasem.

[20] Certain grounds of inadmissibility, including most security-related grounds, cannot be waived.

[21] P.L. 110-293, Title III, §305, July 30, 2008.

[22] U.S. Department of Health and Human Services, Centers for Disease Control and Prevention, "Medical Examination of Aliens—Removal of Human Immunodeficiency Virus (HIV) Infection From Definition of Communicable Disease of Public Health Significance," 74 Federal Register, pp. 56547-56562, November 2, 2009.

[23] See archived CRS Report RL32564, Immigration: Terrorist Grounds for Exclusion and Removal of Aliens, by Michael John Garcia and Ruth Ellen Wasem.

[24] P.L. 110-161, Division J, Title VI, §691, December 26, 2007. DHS and DOS followed this enactment with a series of Federal Register notices similarly stating that the terrorism-related grounds of inadmissibility would generally be waived with respect to any assistance provided by an alien to any of the entities expressly exempted by the Consolidated Appropriations Act, 2008, from being deemed terrorist organizations. U.S. Department of Homeland Security, Office of the Secretary, and Department of State, Office of the Secretary, "Exercise of Authority Under Section 212(d)(3)(B)(i) of the Immigration and Nationality Act" [10 separate notices with same title], 73 Federal Register 34770-34777, June 18, 2008.

[25] P.L. 101-167, Title V, §599D and §599E, November 21, 1989. Parole is a temporary authorization to enter the United States and is typically granted when the alien's entry is determined to be in the public interest.

[26] P.L. 108-199, Division E, Title II, §213, January 23, 2004.

[27] P.L. 111-117, Division F, Title VII, §7034(f), December 16, 2009. Earlier extensions were included in P.L. 108-447, December 8, 2004; P.L. 109-102, November 14, 2005; P.L. 110-5, February 15, 2007; and P.L. 110-161, December 26, 2007.

[28] P.L. 112-10, Division B, §2121(m), April 15, 2011.

[29] P.L. 112-74, Division I, §7034(r), December 23, 2011; P.L. 113-6, Division F, §1706(h), March 26, 2013.

[30] Section 584 of P.L. 104-208, Division A, Section 101(c), September 30, 1996.

[31] P.L. 106-113, Appendix G, Division A, §255, November 29, 1999.

[32] P.L. 107-185, May 30, 2002.

[33] It was extended by P.L. 108-447, P.L. 109-102, and P.L. 110-161.

[34] P.L. 111-8, Division H, §7034(d), March 11, 2009.

[35] P.L. 111-117, Division F, §7034(d).

[36] P.L. 113-6, Division F, §1509.

[37] U.S. Department of Health and Human Services, Administration for Children and Families, ACF All-Purpose Table, 2012-2013, http://www.acf.hhs.gov/programs/olab/resource/administration-for-children-and-families-all-purpose-tablefy-2012-2013.

[38] INA §412(e)(1) authorizes ORR to reimburse states for RCA and RMA for 36 months. Initially, beginning in April 1980, RCA and RMA were available for the full 36 months. As appropriations levels decreased in subsequent years, however, the period of coverage was reduced. Since October 1991, RCA and RMA have been available to refugees for eight months after entry.

[39] For additional discussion of ORR assistance, see archived CRS Report R41570, *U.S. Refugee Resettlement Assistance*, by Andorra Bruno.

[40] The 1996 welfare reform law is the Personal Responsibility and Work Opportunity Reconciliation Act, P.L. 104-193, August 22, 1996.

In: Refugees Around the World
Editor: Jarod Humphrey

ISBN: 978-1-63117-896-2
© 2014 Nova Science Publishers, Inc.

Chapter 3

U.S. REFUGEE ADMISSIONS PROGRAM FAQs[*]

U.S. Department of State, Bureau of Population, Refugees, and Migration

INTRODUCTION

Every year, the United States provides resettlement opportunities to thousands of the world's most vulnerable refugees, in a program endorsed by the President (and every President since 1980) through an annual determination. The U.S. Refugee Admissions Program (USRAP), which resettled over 58,000 refugees in the United States in 2012, reflects our own tradition as a nation of immigrants and refugees. It is an important, enduring and ongoing expression of our commitment to international humanitarian principles. The United States remains the largest resettlement country in the world, receiving more than half of all refugees resettled worldwide each year through the United Nations High Commissioner for Refugees (UNHCR).

The Bureau of Population, Refugees, and Migration (PRM) is committed to improving the effectiveness of the U.S. Refugee Admissions Program, and regularly assesses refugee populations worldwide to ensure that the program is responsive to the resettlement needs of the most vulnerable among them that require this solution.

---

[*] This is an edited, reformatted and augmented version of a Fact Sheet, dated May 31, 2013.

WHO EXACTLY IS ELIGIBLE FOR RESETTLEMENT?

The *United Nations High Commissioner for Refugees* (UNHCR) has the international mandate to provide refugee assistance and to determine if resettlement in a third country - be it the United States or another country - is the right solution.

Less than one percent of refugees worldwide are ever resettled in a third country. UNHCR uses six criteria to determine if resettlement is appropriate. For more information on UNHCR standards and criteria for determining resettlement as the appropriate solution for refugees, please refer to the UNHCR Resettlement Handbook, available online at http://www.unhcr.org/4a2ccf4c6.html.

TELL ME MORE ABOUT HOW THE RESETTLEMENT PROGRAM WORKS

The UNHCR, a U.S. Embassy, or an authorized non-governmental organization (NGO) can refer a refugee to the U.S. Refugee Admissions Program (USRAP). Once a referral is made, a Resettlement Support Center (RSC) funded and managed by PRM prepares the case for presentation to the U.S. Department of Homeland Security (DHS).

The RSC helps the refugee and his/her family (if applicable) prepare their case file - taking photos, checking the facts in the files, collecting information for the security clearance process, etc. Applicants are then interviewed by an officer of DHS' United States Citizenship and Immigration Services (USCIS).

The interviewer adjudicates the case. If approved, the applicant and his/her family undergo medical exams, which are standard for all applicants seeking to reside permanently in the United States.

A non-governmental organization (NGO) working under agreement with PRM in the U.S. then agrees to be the refugee's sponsor. Refugees approved for admission are offered a short cultural orientation program to introduce them to life in the United States. Once all security and health checks are complete, refugees are scheduled for travel to the US.

How Much Time Does the Entire Process Typically Require?

Worldwide, the average processing time is about one year to 18 months. But every case is different, and processing times vary.

How Do You Decide Who Gets in to the United States Under This Program and Who Doesn't?

The Department of Homeland Security has the authority to make this decision. Under U.S. law, a refugee must have a well-founded fear of persecution based on one of the five "protected grounds":

- Religion
- Political opinion
- Race
- Nationality
- Membership in a particular social group

Furthermore, a refugee must be deemed admissible to the U.S. and not be firmly resettled in a third country. For a list of grounds that would disqualify a refugee from resettling in the United States, please visit the U.S. Citizenship and Immigration Services website at *http://www.uscis.gov/portal/site/uscis.*

Is My Nuclear and/or Extended Family Eligible to Join Me?

Generally a "case" consists of the principal applicant, his or her spouse, and unmarried children under the age of 21. Additional relatives may be considered on a case by case basis.

Once a refugee arrives in the United States and would like to petition for other members of his/her immediate family to join them, a number of avenues are available. Under Priority Three (P-3) processing, a refugee or asylee who is at least 18, and been in the U.S. in refugee or asylee status for no more than five years can file an Affidavit of Relationship (AOR) for a spouse, parents, and unmarried children under the age of 21. This form must be submitted to the Department of State through a resettlement agency affiliate in the refugee's geographic area. This program is only open to designated nationalities, set by the Bureau in consultation with DHS/USCIS at the beginning of each fiscal year. DNA testing refugees/asylees and certain family members overseas is a requirement of this program. The P-3 program has been operating since October 15, 2012 following a four year suspension of the program after high rates of relationship fraud were discovered. A refugee who has arrived in the United States, or a person granted asylum in the United States, can also file a Form I-730 (Visa 93) for spouse and unmarried children under the age of 21. There are no restrictions on nationalities that can file this petition, but it must be filed with USCIS within two years of arrival in the United States. The Form I-730 may be downloaded from the USCIS website (www.uscis.gov) and can be submitted directly to USCIS without the aid of a resettlement agency. However, a refugee may consult with a resettlement agency in his/her geographic location for details about this program.

Lastly, a refugee has the option of filing a Form I-130 Petition for Alien Relative upon arrival in the United States. However, only U.S. citizens or refugees with Permanent Resident Alien status are eligible to file this petition. Depending on their legal status in the U.S. applicants may apply on behalf of spouses, children, parents, and siblings. Please visit the USCIS website for eligibility requirements and filing instructions.

WHAT IF SOMEONE IN MY FAMILY DOESN'T GET THE VISA? CAN HE OR SHE REAPPLY?

Approved refugees do not get visas. They receive a packet of documents and information that allows them to enter the U.S.

Anyone whose resettlement application is denied can request that DHS reconsider his/her case.

IF I GO TO THE U.S. AS A REFUGEE, DO I AUTOMATICALLY BECOME A U.S. CITIZEN?

No. Refugees are admitted to the U.S. as refugees and remain in that status for 12 months. They are, however, authorized and expected to work during this time. After 12 months, they are required to adjust their status to that of Permanent Resident Alien. They can apply for citizenship after having been resident in the United States for five years.

WHAT BENEFITS DO I GET IN THE US?

For more information about the State Department Refugee Reception and Placement Program, and what is expected of new arrivals, please click the Refugee Admissions Reception and Placement Program (http://www. state.gov/j/prm/releases/factsheets/2011/181029.htm). For more information on Department of Health and Human Services (HHS) administered refugee benefits, please visit the HHS website (http://www.acf.hhs.gov/programs/orr).

INDEX

J

K

L

M